The original multi-role combat aircraft

UNDOUBTEDLY one of the greatest and most versatile aircraft of World War Two, the Mosquito was also the world's first true multi-role combat aircraft (the second not arriving until the Panavia Tornado). Designed by a company with no previous experience in producing high-performance military aircraft, de Havilland managed to produce a timeless classic which will remain one of those spine-tingling machines now sorely missed in British skies. However, far away in New Zealand, Glyn Powell, and his team at Mosquito Aircraft Restorations, in close collaboration with Avspecs Ltd in Ardmore have been rebuilding a succession of Mosquitos to airworthy condition using newly moulded wooden fuselages.

The Mosquito's versatility during World War Two saw the aircraft operating in a variety of roles including as a pure unarmed bomber, a heavily armed fighter-bomber, rocket, and heavy cannon armed anti-shipping aircraft, radar-equipped night-fighter, an unarmed reconnaissance aircraft, meteorological, trainer and finally as a target tug. From the PR.1 to the T.43, there was not a role the Mosquito could not be adapted to carry out; the aircraft was even modified for light transport work both during and after the war.

What also set the Mosquito apart from the rest was that it performed every role well.

The combination of a superb aircraft and a good crew, of which there were many, saw the Mosquito reach legendary status during its service; this was not an accolade that was placed upon it by post-war historians. The raids that the Mosquito took part in broke all records for distance, time and bomb load, not to mention the accuracy with which they were delivered. Flown by RAF and Commonwealth crews in the skies over Europe, the Mediterranean and the Far East, the Mosquito was a vital cog in the machine that achieved victory against the Axis powers.

The majority of Mosquitos were built in Britain, but mention should also be given to the aircraft built in Australia and Canada which contributed to the grand total of 7,781 delivered. Built in 40 different versions, the Mosquito remained in production from August 1941 through to 1950. It would take something very special to replace the Mosquito in the RAF inventory but luckily another classic came along to take over the reins in the shape of the Canberra, an aircraft which adopted the basic design principles of the de Havilland bomber in more ways than one.

Jerry Yagen's Virginia Beach-based Mosquito FB.26 KA114 (first flying after rebuild on September 28, 2012) wears the EG-Y codes of a No.487 Squadron FB.VI. *Andy Hay/www.flyingart.co.uk*

Cover image: Mosquito NF.11 of No.25 Squadron (DZ685) flown by Flight Lieutenant Joseph 'Joe' Singleton and Flying Officer W G Haslam achieving the squadron's first Mosquito kill – a Ju 88 of KG40. The action took place over the Bay of Biscay on June 11, 1943 while on an Instep patrol. See page 54. *Original artwork by Antonis Karidis for Key Publishing*

This page: Mosquito T.III RR299 and its crew were lost at the Barton Air Show July 21, 1996, but the aircraft is seen here in happier times while serving with 3 CAACU at Exeter, prior to the filming of *633 Squadron. Via Martyn Chorlton*

Originally published 2012 as part of Aeroplane Icons series, updated and republished 2023. Contains minor amendments

ISBN: 978 1 83632 148 4
Author: Martyn Chorlton
Updates: Jon Lake and Paul Hamblin
Senior editor, specials: Roger Mortimer
Email: roger.mortimer@keypublishing.com
Cover Design: Steve Donovan
Design: Dan Jarman and SJmagic DESIGN SERVICES, India
Advertising Sales Manager: Sam Clark
Email: sam.clark@keypublishing.com

Tel: 01780 755131
Advertising Production:
Becky Antoniades
Email: rebecca.antoniades@keypublishing.com

SUBSCRIPTION/MAIL ORDER
Key Publishing Ltd, PO Box 300, Stamford, Lincs, PE9 1NA
Tel: 01780 480404
Subscriptions email: subs@keypublishing.com
Mail Order email: orders@keypublishing.com
Website: www.keypublishing.com/shop

PUBLISHING
Group CEO: Adrian Cox
Publisher: Steve O'Hara

Published by
Key Publishing Ltd, PO Box 100, Stamford, Lincs, PE9 1XQ
Tel: 01780 755131
Website: www.keypublishing.com

PRINTING
Precision Colour Printing Ltd, Haldane, Halesfield 1, Telford, Shropshire. TF7 4QQ

DISTRIBUTION
Seymour Distribution Ltd, 2 Poultry Avenue, London, EC1A 9PU
Enquiries Line: 02074 294000.

Contents

W4050

The Grand Old Lady of Salisbury Hall

The world's only surviving World War Two aircraft prototype was also the first to have been ordered 'straight off the drawing-board'. Martyn Chorlton tells the story of the birth of 'The Wooden Wonder'.

The birth of the Mosquito

During the interwar years, de Havilland had made a name for itself in the field of civilian aviation, designing and building a succession of impressive and successful aircraft. However, by the late 1930s, with the clouds of war again gathering over Europe, Geoffrey de Havilland, with Charles Clement Walker (a founding director and chief engineer) and all of the company's directors began to plan for the approaching conflict. Throughout the summer of 1938, a host of military projects were considered. Most of these were high speed bomber concepts, initially evolved from the established DH.91 Albatross airliner. A bomber version of the Albatross was the most feasible of all of the suggestions put forward within the company. The aircraft was expected to carry a 6,000lb bomb load to Berlin at a speed of 210mph. This idea was refined further with a narrower fuselage before it was finally agreed that an even smaller aircraft, powered by a pair of Rolls-Royce Merlins and with a crew of no more than two, would still be able to carry the same bomb load, considerably faster, and without the need for any defensive armament.

Built from wood

Another crucial decision made at an early stage was that de Havilland's new bomber should be of wooden construction, following the examples of the DH.88 Comet Racer and the Albatross, which had pioneered some very advanced construction methods. It was calculated that building a wooden aircraft would save up to twelve months in the manufacturing, testing and development of the prototype, while De Havilland was also well aware that the supply of aircraft grade aluminium would become critical, and that an aircraft programme that made minimal use of this valuable resource would be strategically valuable.

When the Prime Minister, Neville Chamberlain, returned from signing the Munich Agreement of September 30, 1938, de Havilland stepped up a gear with their new design. The following month, de Havilland presented its proposal for a new wooden bomber to the Air Ministry, only to receive a lukewarm response. De Havilland was not put off and continued further design studies, as well as 'informal' talks with senior members inside the government and Air Ministry. No further progress was made until September 1939 when, as anticipated, Britain again found itself at war with Germany.

De Havilland took the opportunity to put its proposal to the Air Ministry once again, more confident that it would be accepted after the earlier 'informal' talks. A great deal of official scrutiny then followed, and particular concern was expressed about the lack of defensive weapons. Consideration was given to adding remotely operated defensive guns, a rear turret and even an air gunner but Air Marshal Sir Wilfrid Freeman, the Air Member for Development and Production, managed to get the requirement for defensive weapons (and a three man crew) dropped, once it was realised that the unarmed two-seat bomber would comfortably outperform then-current enemy types.

Bomber Command were initially unwilling to accept an unarmed bomber but did leave open the prospect of adapting the design for reconnaissance missions using F8 or F24 cameras.

On December 29, 1939, following another conference and inspection of a full-scale mock-up, de Havilland was ordered to proceed with a single unarmed prototype, though many within the RAF labelled the new machine 'Freeman's Folly'.

The Air Ministry requirement for the new bomber laid down that the new aircraft was to be capable of 400 mph at 18,000 ft, and to have a minimum bomb load of 1,000lb, a range of no less than 1,500 miles and the handling of a fighter.

Salisbury Hall

To maintain secrecy and avoid distractions, the design team, led by R E Bishop, set up shop at Salisbury Hall, a country house just

Geoffrey de Havilland Jr. with observer John E Walker by his side, takes the prototype Mosquito E0234 into the air for the first time from Hatfield on November 25, 1940. *British Aerospace via Aeroplane*

over four miles south of Hatfield. By this time, the new aircraft was designated as the de Havilland DH.98.

Separate interest was also shown in a photographic reconnaissance variant and, to bolster the potential of the aircraft, de Havilland representatives also offered up the idea of a long-range fighter version. The latter did not receive a great deal of enthusiasm at the time but this was catered for from a very early stage and the designers made sure that the basic aircraft all had room for a quartet of 20mm cannon under the cockpit floor.

Incredibly, on March 1, 1940, with the prototype still several months away from flying, the director-general of research and development, Air Marshal Roderic Hill issued a contract for 50 bomber-reconnaissance variants of the DH.98 straight off the drawing board. These included the prototype, and were to conform to Specification B.1/40 to fulfil OR.78 – the RAF's ambitious requirement for an unarmed twin-engined fast bomber. At this time, Britain was still fighting the so-called 'Phoney War', with France yet to fall. The order was small, by Air Ministry standards, mainly because it was realised that very different types of aircraft could be required depending on how the war progressed. Two months later, in May 1940, the Air Ministry issued specification F.21/40 for a long-range fighter armed with four 20 mm cannon and four .303 machine guns in the nose. De Havilland was soon authorised to build a prototype of the fighter version of the DH.98, to be equipped with airborne interception (AI) Mk IV radar equipment.

Following the evacuation of Dunkirk, Lord Beaverbrook became the Minister of Aircraft Production in the new Churchill government. Churchill was keen that all of the nation's aircraft manufacturers should concentrate on building aircraft to meet current operational requirements and Beaverbrook decided that there was no spare production capacity for aircraft like the DH.98, which was not expected to be in service until early 1942. Beaverbrook told Freeman that work on the project should stop, but the RAF officer ignored the request. In June 1940, however, Lord Beaverbrook and the Air Staff ordered that work on the DH.98 prototype be stopped to allow production to concentrate on the Supermarine Spitfire, Hawker Hurricane, Vickers Wellington, Armstrong-Whitworth Whitley, and Bristol Blenheim. This was where the Mosquito story could have come to an end but for the tenacity of De Havilland. The materials they needed to continue with the B.1/40 were made available again in July 1940, by which time the aircraft had been named as the Mosquito.

Work on the Mosquito was only reinstated after Beaverbrook had been reassured that Mosquito production would not get in the way of de Havilland's priority work of producing Tiger Moth and Airspeed Oxford trainers, repairing battle-damaged Hurricanes, and manufacturing Merlin engines under licence.

Bombers, fighters, single or dual?

While the original order for 50 aircraft was to be honoured, it was amended to cover the production of 20 bombers and 30 fighters. Three fighter prototypes were included, two of them intended to be equipped with gun turrets and dual controls. These would eventually emerge as T.Mk III trainer prototypes. There was a slight delay in production because the fighter needed to be built with a stronger main spar. At Hatfield, 28 forward fuselage sections had already been completed and all had to be modified into fighter versions.

Construction of the very first Mosquito progressed through the autumn of 1940 and was delayed only by a succession of German air raids. One particular raid on Hatfield on October 3, 1940 by a single Junkers Ju88 was the only instance when progress was seriously disrupted. The enemy bomber dropped four bombs which skidded on the wet grass and exploded in a sheet metal shop, destroying 80% of the

The elegant lines and innovative construction of the DH.91 Albatross airliner provided inspiration for de Havilland's high-speed bomber concepts. *Via author*

The unique sight of the world's only airworthy DH.88 Comet (at the time) G-ACSS in company with the British Aerospace-operated Mosquito T.III, RR299. RR299 was destroyed in a fatal accident in July 1996, while the Comet remains with the Shuttleworth Collection having been restored to airworthiness in 2014, after flying just once since 1994. *Via author*

Mosquito working materials (the equivalent of nine month's work), killing 21 workers and wounding 70 more. Despite the setback, de Havilland's general manager, L C L Murray, had promised Lord Beaverbrook 50 Mosquitos by December 1941.

First flight from Hatfield

The prototype Mosquito was built in a small hangar, disguised as a barn, outside Salisbury Hall. At this stage, the aircraft was painted bright 'prototype yellow' (purely to aid anti-aircraft gunners in the aircraft's recognition) and given the Class B serial of E0234. The aircraft was then dismantled and, on November 3, 1945, made the short journey by road to Hatfield, heavily disguised under a tarpaulin. On arrival at Hatfield, the Mosquito was delivered to a small blast-proof building where the task of re-assembling the aircraft was undertaken.

The aircraft's twin Merlin 21 two-speed, single-stage supercharged engines were installed and were ground run on November 19. Five days later the aircraft undertook taxi

tests for the first time. On November 25, at 1545hrs, the prototype Mosquito made its maiden flight in the hands of Geoffrey de Havilland Jr and John E Walker, de Havilland's chief engine installation designer. The first flight was a remarkable achievement taking place just short of 11 months after detailed design work had been given the go ahead.

The Mosquito only flew twice with the serial E0234 and, from then on, was given the military serial W4050. The aircraft instantly caused a stir at Hatfield with its impressive performance, which was twice as fast as anything that had been built by the company previously. It took just three months and 35 hours of flying time to complete the manufacturer's trials, by which time the Mosquito had been confirmed as the world's fastest combat aircraft. It would hold this title for two and half years. Very few minor modifications resulted from these early trials.

Testing at Boscombe Down

On February 19, 1941, W4050 was delivered to the Aeroplane & Armament Experimental

Establishment (A&AEE) at Boscombe Down for Performance and Handling trials. On arrival, the colour scheme had been toned down somewhat with camouflaged upper surfaces and traditional prototype 'P' markings on the sides of the rear fuselage.

This first visit to the A&AEE was cut short when, on February 24 after just eight and half hours of flight testing, mainly by test pilot Allen Wheeler, the rear fuselage failed on landing, fracturing behind the trailing edge of the wing and suffering Category 4 damage. On this occasion, the aircraft was being flown by Flt Lt C E Slee and observer AC Jay of 'C' Flight, Performance Test Squadron, A&AEE. The aircraft was being assessed at a weight of 16,770lb without 'armament or other operational equipment and was only lightly loaded'.

The incident was blamed on the tailwheel jamming in a rut due to castoring difficulties. A similar tail wheel-related incident was destined to befall the second prototype, W4051, at Boscombe on June 28, 1941.

▲ E0234 pictured on a quiet side of Hatfield during further engine testing on November 21, 1940. *British Aerospace via Aeroplane*

E0234 attracts a great deal of attention during its first taxi tests, on November 24, 1940. *British Aerospace via Aeroplane* ➤

▲ Early airborne photographs of the prototype Mosquito were not of the highest quality. This is E0234 conducting its second flight from Hatfield on November 29, 1940. *British Aerospace via Aeroplane*

Mosquito E0234 pictured at Hatfield on November 19, 1940 during the aircraft's first engine tests.
Air Ministry via Aeroplane

W4050 was given a temporary repair by de Havilland staff to allow it to be flown back to Hatfield. The aircraft was inspected by de Havilland's chief engineer, Fred Plumb, who decided that it would be easier to replace the entire rear fuselage than to repair it, so W4050 was fitted with the rear fuselage intended for W4051, the prototype reconnaissance variant. This work was completed on March 14 and, following some minor adjustments, W4050 returned to Boscombe on March 18 to continue testing. Apart from its new tail, W4050 had its engine nacelles temporarily extended to the rear which resulted in the flaps having to be locked in the 'up' position.

Extension of the engine nacelles had reduced vibration, a problem that had been pointed out during the first brief trial. The vibration was, at first, incorrectly assumed to have been attributed to the engines but was actually caused by turbulence around the tail and the new engine nacelles had cured this problem. The A&AEE's Initial Handling Report 767 had described the Mosquito as being: 'pleasant to fly' with light and effective aileron control. And it continued, W4050 proved able to outpace a Spitfire – clocking 392 mph at 22,000 ft - where the Mk.II Spitfire achieved just 360 mph at 19,500 ft.

A later report described the aircraft as being much more pleasant to fly, though the subsequent A&AEE report stated that the aircraft was still 'very difficult to trim accurately in level flight'.

Following the completion of the Performance and Handling trials, W4050 returned to Hatfield again. This time, the temporary engine nacelles were replaced with a more permanent modification allowing the flaps, which were now split, to be operated. The elevator balance was also increased, and extra fuel tanks were fitted so that the all-up weight could be increased to the maximum overload of 19,500lb.

On May 3, 1941, W4050 returned to Boscombe for more handling trials. During this period, the aircraft's stability was described as being 'unpleasant in bumps and turns', a problem that was aggravated by the radiator flaps which were thermostatically controlled and would open automatically without any warning to cause 'a sharp change of trim to tail heaviness'. The A&AEE recommended that 'the change of trim is a serious matter which should receive consideration.'

The flaps were a cause for concern as well, being described as rising too rapidly which caused a dramatic change in pitch. This was reported as being unsatisfactory, especially during the approach to land. The A&AEE test pilots and observers also found the cockpit to be 'too hot at low and medium altitudes' and found that fumes entered the cockpit during taxiing. The pilot's seat was also described as being uncomfortable after 11/2 to two hours of flying and the A&AEE recommended tilting the seat back by 10°.

After 20 flights totalling 12hrs 45mins, the rear fuselage failed again. Following the second structural failure, which was repaired on site by a large patch which can still be seen today, W4050 did not appear in any more A&AEE reports.

Other prototypes joined the test effort. W4051 was designed from the outset to be the photo-reconnaissance prototype, but its first flight was delayed when the fuselage fracture in W4050 meant that its fuselage was used as a replacement. The aircraft was then rebuilt using a production standard fuselage and flew on June 10, 1941. W4051 had short engine nacelles, single-piece trailing-edge flaps, and the original tailplane, but was fitted with production-standard 54ft 2in wings and subsequently became the only Mosquito prototype to fly operationally.

Mosquito W4052 was the fighter prototype, and featured a redesigned canopy

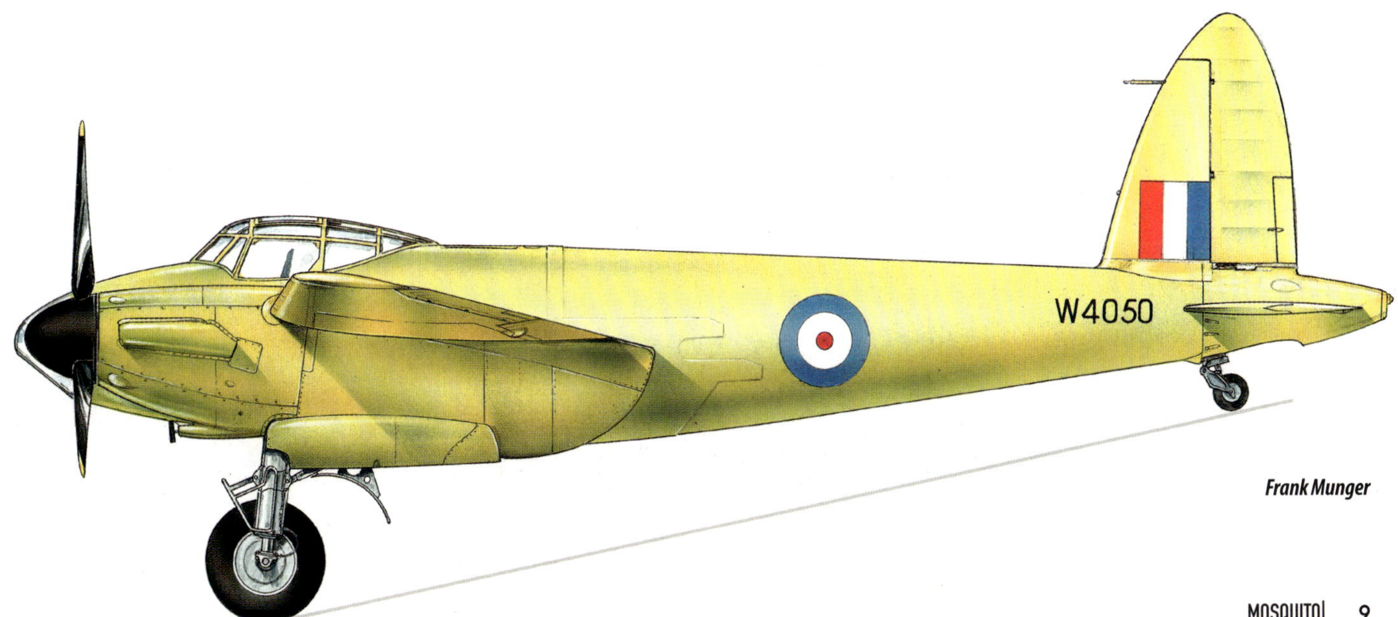

Frank Munger

structure with a flat, bullet-proof windscreen and a solid nose with four .303 British Browning machine guns and their ammunition boxes, while four 20mm Hispano Mk.II cannon were housed in a compartment under the cockpit floor. W4052 was also fitted with AI Mk IV radar equipment, complete with an 'arrowhead' transmitter aerial mounted between the central Brownings and receiver aerials on the wing tips. It was also the first prototype constructed with the extended engine nacelles and was painted in black RDM2a 'Special Night' finish.

Second wind

By late October 1941, W4050 had been re-engined with a pair of Merlin 61s but did not fly again until June 1942. On only its second test flight with the new powerplants, on June 20, W4050 reached 40,000ft with ease. In October 1942 W4050 was grounded again to be re-fitted with extended wingtips, increasing the span to 59ft 2in connection with development work on the NF Mk XV, also gaining a pair of Merlin 77 engines for flight trials. An impressive top speed of 439mph was achieved in November 1942, making the prototype the fastest Mosquito around. Some development flying continued into 1943, but this became less and less, although W4050 did spend a period with Rolls-Royce at Hucknall from March 1 to June 10. There were plans for W4050 to be scrapped and burned, but instead she served as an instructional airframe with the de Havilland apprentice school at Hatfield.

Grounded

W4050 was briefly back in the public eye in 1945 when the aircraft featured in the film *The Mosquito Story*. The film was made by de Havilland about the design, development, and subsequent service of the Mosquito.

By 1946, W4050 found itself back at Salisbury Hall, once again as a static airframe for training purposes, this time for the de Havilland Aeronautical School. Many wartime prototypes had already bitten the dust, but the Mosquito prototype was still earning its keep, and appeared in the static display at the SBAC air shows at Radlett in 1946 and 1947.

By the late 1940s, the historical significance of W4050 was in danger of being overlooked and, on June 21, 1947, the aircraft was declared Category E by de Havilland and was again struck off charge, with orders for it to be destroyed. However, the importance of the aircraft had not escaped everyone's attention, and when the assistant public relations manager at Hatfield, W J S 'Bill' Baird, heard about W4050's precarious position, he decided to act. Baird saved W4050 from a fiery end and arranged for the Mosquito to be dismantled and moved to Panshangar aerodrome, until de

Havilland sold that airfield off in 1953. Further moves saw the Mosquito return to Hatfield, then move to Chester before returning to Hatfield again for storage 'off the airfield.'

While W4050 was being shuffled around the country another fortuitous event occurred when a retired army officer by the name of Walter J Goldsmith purchased Salisbury Hall. It was not long before he discovered that it was the birthplace of the Mosquito and, after finding out that the prototype still existed, suggested that it could be displayed at Salisbury Hall. In September 1958, W4050 was returned to the Salisbury Hall hangar where it was built on a Queen Mary trailer. The aircraft was restored to its original configuration and was put on public display on May 15, 1959. She has been on display ever since and is today one of the primary exhibits of the de Havilland Aircraft Heritage Centre. ❖

W4050 at the SBAC at Radlett in 1946, surrounded by an array of drop tanks and weapons, including a torpedo under the fuselage. *Aeroplane* ➤

W4050 pictured in September 1942 fitted with a pair of Merlin 61 engines — the first production Merlins with a two-speed, two-stage supercharger. With these installed the aircraft had reached 40,000ft the previous June. *Via author*

W4050 being painstakingly restored at the de Havilland Aircraft Heritage Centre in the grounds of Salisbury Hall. Since the Mosquito prototype's arrival in 1958, the collection has grown to 30 different aircraft; all but two of them are de Havilland types. ➤

THE DE HAVILLAND
AIRCRAFT CO., LTD.

Hatfield Aerodrome Herts. England

GdeH/ELC

Air Marshal Sir Wilfrid R. Freeman,   20th September 1939.
K.C.B., D.S.O., MC,
Air Member for Development and Production,
Air Ministry,
Berkeley Square House,
Berkeley Square,
LONDON W.1.

Dear Freeman,

We have stopped all civil design and want to put our whole design staff on to war work. From former conversations with you, and using the experience we have gained in very quickly producing types which have to compete with others from all over the world we believe that we could produce a twin engine bomber which would have a performance so outstanding that little defensive equipment would be needed.

This would employ the well tried out methods of design and construction used in the 'COMET` and the ALBATROSS` and, being of wood or composite construction, would not encroach on the labour and material used in expanding the RAF. It is specially suited to really high speeds because all surfaces are smooth, free from rivets, overlapped plates and undulations. It also lends itself to very rapid initial and subsequent production.

The brief specification would be as follows:

Rolls-Royce Merlin 100 octane engines.
1,500 miles range.
Two 500 lb. or six 250 lb. bombs.
Pilot and observer.
Maximum speed 405 m.p.h. at 20,000 feet.
Cruise on weak mixture 320 m.p.h.
Take-off would be well within the extended limits allowed for bombers.
Landing without fuel and bombs would be on a wing loading of 30 lbs. per sq. ft.

The principal objects which would be achieved by this type are shortly as follows:-

1. Its production would absorb a class of labour and material which is outside and additional to that used in the main aircraft production.
2. The smallest possible call would be made on 'Embodiment Loan` stuff etc., owing to its simplicity and to the fact that it relies mainly on performance for its defences.
3. It makes use of a design staff which has had much experience in very quickly producing aircraft types to meet specific and competitive needs.
4. The wood or composite construction allows of the minimum time and man-hours being spent on making jigs etc.
5. The existence of a type of bomber having the highest performance possible and capable within a year of going into production forms a kind of insurance against surprises emanating from the enemy`s design resources. If a prototype were undergoing trials in, say, nine months, without detracting from the main production plans, it would be a platform for future plans, the value of which can hardly be exaggerated.
6. This type of construction permits mixed grades of timber to be used with safety.

We have arranged a provincial location and are moving our design staff to it. We should be able therefore, to start on this project forthwith.

We feel such confidence that the existence of this type or a closely similar one will be a valuable asset in a year`s time that we very much hope you will be able to give it your support. If this is the case we should have to discuss the minimum equipment with the people concerned.

Yours sincerely,

(Signed) G. de Havilland

P.S. I am anxious to get this preliminary proposal in to you without delay, but will just add that it has been based on the availability of Merlin engines. Were it possible to use Sabres the same performance and range could be obtained with 4,000 lbs. of bombs, crew of three and two guns.

W4050, which thanks to its preservation during the 1950s, is the world's oldest surviving Mosquito and additionally one of the world's oldest surviving prototypes. *Aeroplane*

W4051

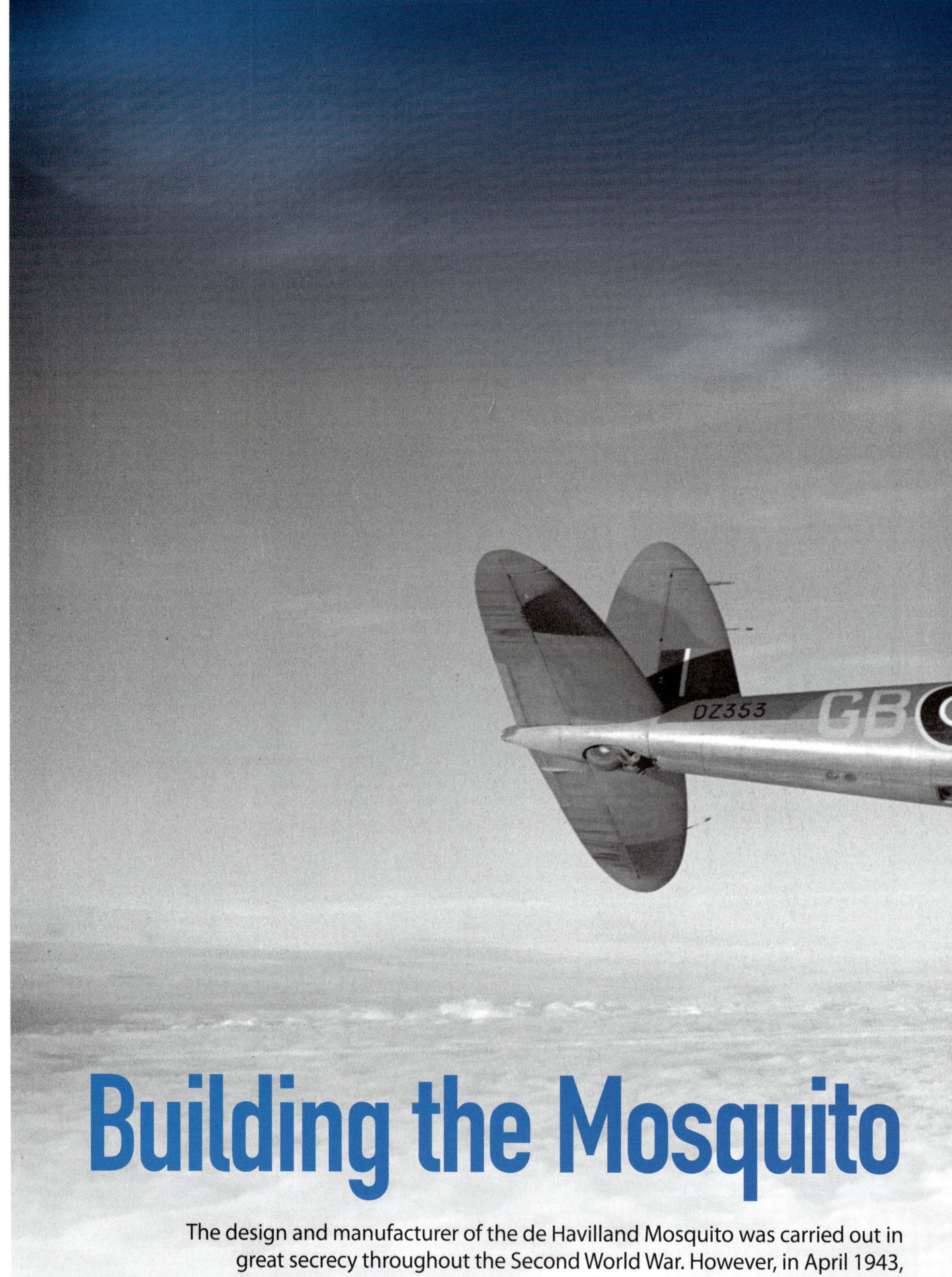

Building the Mosquito

The design and manufacturer of the de Havilland Mosquito was carried out in great secrecy throughout the Second World War. However, in April 1943, *The Aeroplane* was invited to Hatfield (the location could not be revealed at the time) where the following report and superb photographs were taken.

The 344th Mosquito to be built was B.IV DZ353, pictured here during its service with 105 Squadron at Marham. The bomber went on to serve with 139 and then 627 Squadron until it went missing on an operation to Rennes on June 9, 1944. *Aeroplane*

The fuselage of the Mosquito was built in two halves, making the fitment of internal equipment much easier. This is a Mosquito B.IV, the construction number (c/n) 524 chalked and stencilled giving away the aircraft's later identity as DZ595 destined to serve with 105 Squadron. *Aeroplane*

The two halves of c/n 507 (B.IV DZ578) have been fitted out with internal equipment, hydraulic pipe-work and wires and cables just prior to being glued together. *Aeroplane*

At least 50 unidentified Mosquito fuselages on the Hatfield production line are visible here, being produced six abreast from the second row back. *Aeroplane*

Outdistancing in all pursuit

THE FASTEST AEROPLANE of any type in operation with any air force in the World today - that is the proud distinction of the de Havilland Mosquito with its two Rolls-Royce Merlin engines. Just how fast the Mosquito is we may not mention yet. What can be said is that a Mosquito bomber, with 2,000lb of bombs and enough fuel to fly to Berlin and back, is faster than any fighter in service today. Its long-range capabilities are well illustrated by the fact that Mosquitos have flown from the British Isles to Russia in time for lunch and back again the same afternoon.

Thus for the second time in two wars, a de Havilland bomber has been produced which can out distance all pursuit. The Mosquito - the D.H.98 - is a direct descendant from the D.H.4 of 1917. That early de Havilland day bomber with a 375h.p. Rolls-Royce Eagle VIII motor achieved 143mph compared with the 135mph of the fastest contemporary fighter.

Not only is the Mosquito the fastest aeroplane in service, but it also holds the record for progress from initial drawings to active operation against the enemy. Today its production is the most widely dispersed of any operational aeroplane, both in England where it is being assembled in several depots and built by more than 400 sub-contractors, and also in Canada.

Design

Aerodynamically, all the Mosquitos are two-motor, high mid-wing monoplanes, with fully retractable undercarriage and single fin and rudder. The radiators are mounted in the centre-section of the wing between the fuselage and the engine nacelles, where they offer remarkably little drag.

Structurally, the Mosquito is built almost entirely of wood. The wings are of stressed-skin wooden construction. The fuselage is

Two halves of the fuselage are bonded together with the help of metal braces around the rear fuselage, various clamps and a large metal jig in the centre where the wing will be fitted. *Aeroplane*

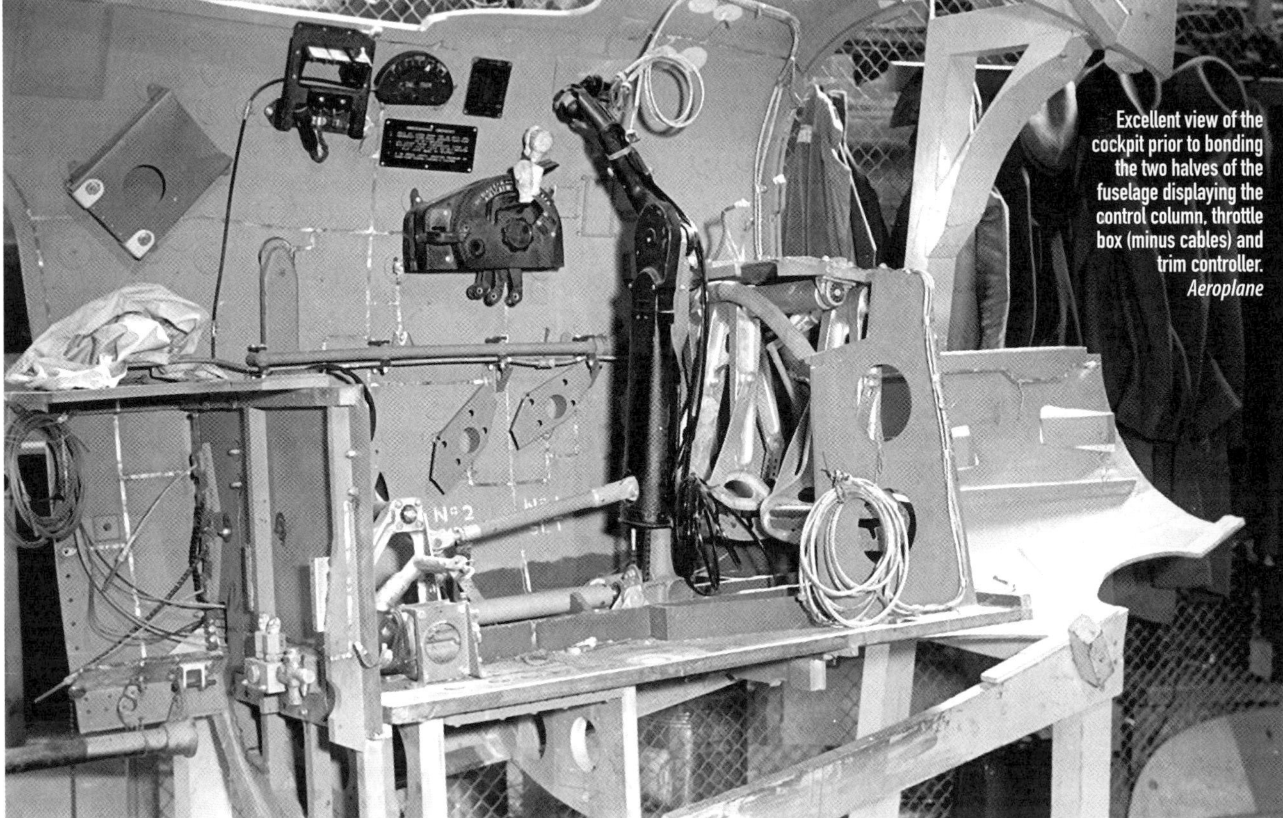

Excellent view of the cockpit prior to bonding the two halves of the fuselage displaying the control column, throttle box (minus cables) and trim controller. *Aeroplane*

similar to that of the Albatross except that it is assembled in two halves, split along the longitudinal axis from nose to tail, top and bottom. This feature makes installation of equipment remarkably easy.

Three primary reasons governed the decision to adopt wood for construction:

(i) For quickness of design and to get the prototype into production as soon as possible.

(ii) To tap materials not being fully used.

(iii) To employ new labour.

At the time when the production of the Mosquito began there were said to be some 12,000 skilled woodworkers unemployed. Furthermore, use of wood made possible greater dispersal of production, greater ease of repair and increased buoyancy should a forced descent on the water be necessary.

Another factor which has proved valuable in wood construction is the surface finish which can be secured. In these days of camouflage paint this might not be considered of much importance, especially as a 'velvet' black night-flying coat was found to reduce the speed by about 16mph without

any further alteration. But the smoothness of the skin, free from rivets or ripples, helps greatly to maintain performance at high speeds.

When the design was begun, little was known about how wooden construction would withstand enemy fire, except for the experience of 1914-18. The results in service have been most enlightening. Bullets or fragments of AA or cannon shell go through the structure like a knife through cheese. They usually emerge the other side, leaving holes little bigger than the missiles. And because wood is bulkier than metal for the same

▲ The fully bonded fuselage is now ready to be fitted with more equipment and control cables, in this instance, the cockpit receives the necessary instruments, while electrical wires and hydraulic cables trail to the rear in readiness for the wing and power plants. *Aeroplane*

The upper centre section of a Mosquitoe's wing takes shape at a very early stage of the construction. *Aeroplane* ➤

Mounted in a vertical jig, the wing was constructed in one piece, making it particularly strong. A Hatfield wood-worker fits clamps around the spanwise formers during the bonding process. *Aeroplane* ▼

strength, the bullet holes are a smaller proportion of the total and so weaken the structure less. Repairs are comparatively easy by any skilled carpenter. Even a damaged wingtip can be cut off and a new section butt-jointed into place, a valuable feature in war.

Thus wood construction has many advantages, and for a company such as de Havilland, which has had long experience in woodwork for aircraft, wood became a natural choice.

Wings

The wings of the Mosquito are built up in a single section from tip to tip. The centre portion carries the radiator and engine mountings. The fuselage drops on top of the centre section and is secured by four massive pick-up points.

There are two box spars with ply webs and laminated spruce flanges. The front spar has three laminations at the top and eleven at the bottom. The rear spar has three laminations at the top but only nine at the bottom. The skin passes right across the top and bottom of the spars and is of double thickness on top with spanwise spruce stringers sandwiched between two diagonal layers of ply.

A false leading edge is attached to the front spar and is of conventional built-up construction. The whole of the wing is screwed, glued and pinned and then covered with fabric on top of the ply.

The wings are severely tapered at the

▲ Production did not stop during *The Aeroplane's* visit to Hatfield in 1943, not a single worker in this photo is pausing to look at the camera whilst working on this Mosquito wing. *Aeroplane*

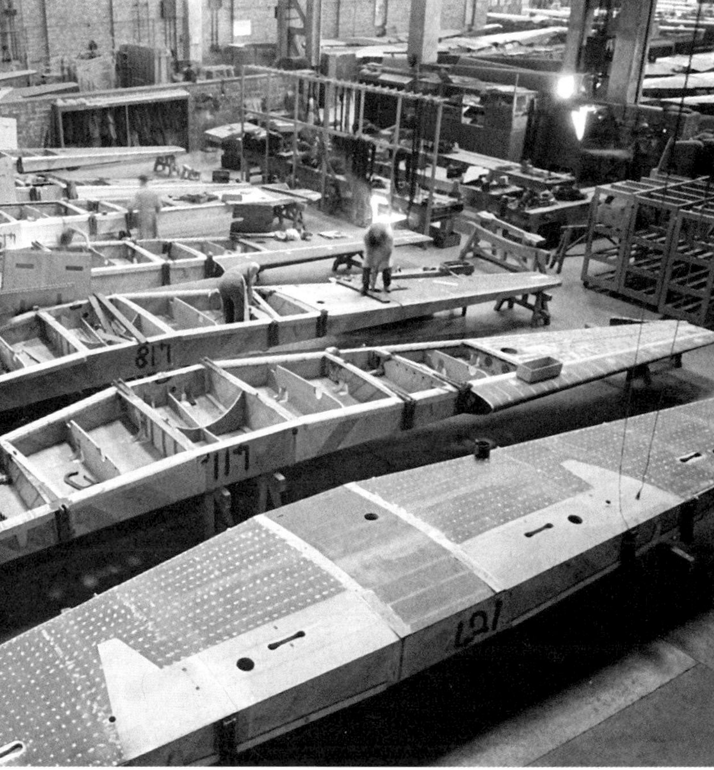

◀ The undersides of seven sets of wings progress from the top to the bottom of the photograph. By the time the wing reaches the bottom of the image, the plywood under-skins are fixed into place and inspection doors are marked out for cutting. Three of these wings are marked c/n 411, 418 and 421 (B.IVs, DZ435, DZ442 and DZ460 respectively). *Aeroplane*

trailing edge but only slightly swept back at the leading edge. The ailerons, 12ft 5in long, extend almost from the tip to the large-chord slotted flap which extends inboard to the nacelle and then from nacelle to fuselage.

Fuselage

Mosquito fuselages are built in two halves on two half-jigs, the split being along the top and bottom from nose to tail. The two halves for each aeroplane are built at the same time, so that temperature variations affect both halves equally. They stay together throughout the whole process of assembly until they are finally joined together. They are not interchangeable.

Construction follows the lines of that of the Albatross. The fuselage has a sandwich skin made of an outer layer of ply, a centre of balsa wood and an inner skin of plywood again. At the points where the bulkheads are attached, the balsa core is omitted and a spruce ring substituted. The skin varies in thickness from 1.5 millimetres to 3.0 millimetres.

There are seven bulkheads in all from nose to tail. Each is built up of two plywood skins kept apart by spruce blocks.

Wherever the skin is most stressed, the plywood skin is wrapped on diagonally. Where strength is not so important it is put on straight so as to use less wood. No attachments are made directly to the skin. Instead, a hole is drilled from the inside through the ply into the balsa and a Bakelite plug with a ply flange is set into the hole and glued in place. The flange of the 'top hat' is glued to the skin and the loads are transmitted through this when a screw is threaded into the Bakelite.

The pick-up points for the wing are made of laminated spruce glued to spruce inserts in the skin and affording a very large bearing are for distributing of the loads.

All the equipment, such as electric leads, oxygen bottles, and starboard segments of the fuselage are scarfed together with Vee notches, a plywood strip is placed over the joint inside and a ply insert outside.

Clamps are put round the fuselage while the joint sets hard. Production is now changing over from casein to beetle glue as the beetle glue is not affected by water and hence has better weathering properties.

When the two halves are assembled the whole fuselage is covered with fabric and doped.

▲ At least 20 sets of Mosquito wings reach their final stage of assembly having been painted and all but the ailerons in place. *Aeroplane*

Detail of tail wheel chain driven control, elevator bar, rudder and trim tab of a factory fresh Mosquito B.IV in silver primer . *Aeroplane* ▼

▲ Flap detail, showing the flap jack and crank prior to being connected. *Aeroplane*

Taking shape. Once the wing is in place, progress is swift as all the wiring and pipework for the twin Merlin engines can be prepared prior to their installation. *Aeroplane* ▼

Mosquito sub-contractors and suppliers

Apart from the large numbers of 'home workers', over 400 contractors, sub-contractors and suppliers had a hand in the making of the Mosquito, in Britain, Canada and Australia. The following list, which is as complete as it is possible to make it, shows the great diversity of industries represented.

(Without exception, every company listed is a Corp. or Co., Ltd or both, this has been removed to save space!)

Accles & Pollock; Acton Bolt; Addis Brush Works; Adrema; Aero Pipe & Glass; Aeroplane & Motor Aluminium Castings; Aircraft Materials; Airworks General Trading; Albion Drop Forgings; Alford & Adler; Alltools (Airframes); Aluminium Plant & Vessel; Amal; Anglo-Cutting Tool; E.S.Aston; Attewill & Sons; Auto-Dairy Engineers; Avimo; Avon India Rubber; Bakelite; Walter F.Baker; Balsa Wood; Barber & Colman; Barker Bros; Barnet Engineering; Barrow Hepburn & Gale; Barter Trading; Baxter (Bolts, Screws & Rivets); B.B. Chemical; Bell & Frome; Belling & Lee; Bell Punch; Benton & Stone; F.W.Berk; Barry, Wiggins; Bifurcated & Tubular River; William Birch; Birche & Alpe; Birmetals; Birmingham Aluminium Castings; Birmingham Guild; J.I.Blackburn; Blackheath Stamping; Bloxwich Lock & Stamping; T.Bolton & Sons; James Booth; Bowden (Engineers); David Bowling; D.H.Bownella & Sons; J.R.Bramah; Bratt Colbran; Bretts Stamping; Briggs Motor Bodies; British Aluminium; British Engraving & Nameplate Manufacturing(London); British Indestructo Glass; British Insulated Callenders

Cables; British Oxygen Gases; British Plywood Manufacturers; British Ropes; British Thomson-Houston; Brooklands Eng.; T.J.Brooks (Autos); Brown Bayley Steel; Brown Bros (Aircraft); Brunt Coaches; Bruntons (Musselburgh); B.T.R. Industries; Bunn; Bushing. Campbell Engineering; Catalin; Cellon; Chater Lea Manufacturing; C.W.Cheney & Sons; Chesterfield Tube; Chillington Tool; W.T.Clark (Metal Spinners) Clavis Tool; Clevedon Rivets & Tools; Chas. Clifford; Clydesdale Stamping; H. Comoy; Compton; Cooper (Birmingham); Cooper & Turner; Co-op Wholesale Society; Cope & Timmins (London) 1911; Courtney-Pope; Covell & Foord; P.B.Cow; Cox; Hilliaam J.Cox; J.H.Crabtree; Cundall Folding Machine; C.V.A.; Dagenham Motors; J.Dale; Daner & Hearne Bros; Dark Spring; Davis & Timmins (Aircraft); Delaney Gallay; Delta Metal; Deritend Drop Forging; Diamond Screw & Cotter; Diecastings; T.H.Dixon; Dudley Drop Forging; Dufay Development; Dunlop Rubber; Dzus Fasteners (Europe); Eagle Transfers; Earle Bourne; Egerton Tool; Elliotts of Newbury; Enfield Cables; English Steel; E.S.A.; Evertaut; Farnworth Engineering; Faulkness; Ferodo; Field Aircraft Services; Fireproof Tanks; Thos. Firth & J.Brown; Firth Vickers Stainless Steels; Fisher & Ludlow; Flexo Plywood Industries; Forgings & Pressworth; S.Fox; Franco-British Electrical; Frigidaire; Geecen; General Electric; General Plastics; Gillette Industries; Glynhir Tinplate; E.Gomme; Gramophone; Guest, Keen & Nettlefold; Hadfields; Hall & Hall; Halladay's Drop Forgings; Hanworth Engineering; Harborough Construction; G.A.Harvey (London); Haskine; T.P.Hawkins & Son; The

Henderson Safety Tank; W.Henshall & Son (Adlestone); Herbert & Sons; Hertfordshire Rubber; Heston Aircraft; High Duty Alloys; J.A.Hillman; E.Hines; Hobbies; Hoffman Manufacturing; Hooper (Coachbuilders); Houdaille; Hughes Johnson Stamping; Hunting Aircraft; Hymatic Engineering; I.C.I.; Insulations Equipment; G.O.James; A.E.Jenks & Cattell; G.K.Jensen; Matthey Johnson; W.Clifton Jones; Kaultex; Kaye Alloy Castings; Kenilworth Manufacturing; Kent Alloys; Kings Langley Engineering; Kiveton Park Steel & Wire Works; Lancefield Aircraft Components; Lancefield Coachworks; Walter Lawrence & Son; Harris Lebus; Arthur Lee & Sons; Leeds Metal Spinners; Leeds Spring; Light Alloys; Light Metal Forgings; Linolite; Linread; Lockheed Hydraulic Brake; London Name-Plate Manufacturing; Lupton & Place; Magnall Products; Manganese Bronze & Brass; Marshall's Flying School; Martin Baker Aircraft; Masson Seeley; H.J.Maybrey; Metalastik; Metal Castings; M.H.H. Engineering; Micanite & Insulator; Midland Repetition & Auto Manufacturing; Mills Equipment; Exors James Mills; M.L.H. Manufacturing; Mollart Engineering; Morgan; Motor Panels (Coventry); H.J.Mulliner; A.P.Newall; L.H.Newton; Northern Aluminium; The Nuffield Organisation; Opperman Gears; Ormond Engineering; Page Bros.; Palmer Aero Products; Parker-Knoll; Park Ward; G.Parnall; L.F.Peaty; Perfecta Motor Equipments; H.Perks; Perry Barr Metal; Pianoforte Supplies; Pinchin & Johnson; The Plessey; E.Pollard; W.Potter; Power Flexible Tubing; D.Ponds & Sons; W.H.Pressland & Son; Pytram; Ransome & Maries Bearing; Renns

Shaped Ply; Renold; Reynold Tube; Ripaults; Rodd Engineering; Rolls Royce; Rose Bros (Gainsborough); Rose Courtney; Rotax; Rotherham Forge & Rolling Mills; Rother-ham & Sons; Sadgrove; Geo. Salter; Joseph Sankey & Sons; Saro Laminated Wood Products; W.H.Saunders; Shand Kydd; Shaw & Kilburn; Sherwood Paints; Siemens Edison Swan; Simmond's Aerocessories; Singer Motors; Skefco Ball Bearing; Smethwick Drop Forgings; Smiths Aircraft Instruments; Smiths Stamping Works (Coventry); Sorbo; Southern United Engraving; G.Spencer Moulton; Spring Washers; Stampings Alliance; Standard Motors; Stanley Engineering; Stanley Smith; Steel Nut & Joseph Hampton; Stirling Metals; J.Stone; Swift Levick & Sons; Tankard & Smith; Tecalemit; Teleflex Products; Telegram Construction and Maintenance; Temple Pianoforte; H.Terry & Sons; R.Thomas & Baldwin; Thompson Bros (Bilston); W.L.Thurgood; W.H.Tildesley; Titanine; Triplex Safety Glass; Tube Products; Tubes; Geo. Tucker Eyelet; Tungum; G.Turton Platts; Universal Mat; Vanden Plas; Vatric (Precision Tools); Vaughan Bros (Drop Forgings); Vauxhall Motors; Venesta; Victoria Drop Forgings; The Vincent H.R.D.; Vokes; Vowles; Vulcanised Fibres; Warwick Rim & Sectioning; Eustace Watkins; Waygood Otis; Weyburn Engineering; Whitaker & Shenton; J.Samuel White; Whiteley Products; D.Wickham; H. Wiggin; W.J.Wild; Wilkinson Rubber Linatex; Willenhall Motor Radiator; Wilmot Breeden; Wilson & Pearce; Wimbush; Wright Ropes; J. Wright & Sons (Veneers); M.Wright & Sons; Wrighton & Sons; H.W.Wylld.

A 1,230hp Rolls-Royce Merlin 21 being installed into a Mosquito B.IV; one of 273 built by de Havilland at Hatfield. *Aeroplane*

Mosquito NF.38 was the 7,781st and last Mosquito built. She is seen outside the production hangar at Chester on November 15, 1950, with some of those who built her. Altogether, 3,299 Mosquitoes were built at Hatfield, 1,627 at Leavesden, 1,134 by DH Canada at Toronto, 1,065 by Standard Motors at Coventry, 245 by Percival Aircraft at Luton, 208 by DH Australia at Sydney, 122 by Airspeed at Christchurch, and 81 at Chester. Out of the totals for the ten years, the figures for the war period were 3,054 at Hatfield; 1,390 at Leavesden; 1,032 by DH Canada; 1,126 by Standard Motors, Percival and Airspeed; and 108 by DH Australia. *Via Aeroplane*

▲ The bomb aimer poses for the camera in the nose of a Mosquito B.IV which has already carried out 20 operations. Many Mosquitoes chalked up more than 100 operations and several breached the 200 barrier as well. *Charles E Brown*

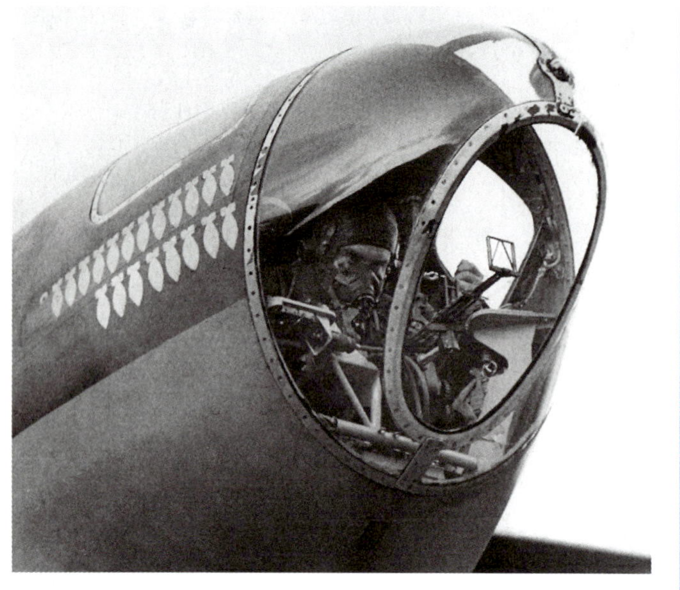

Capable of delivering an attack comparable to an aircraft much bigger, the Mosquito bomber variants could pack a punch from any operational height against any target within 1,000 miles. David H. Smith outlines the multiple bomber variants.

A thorn in Germany's side

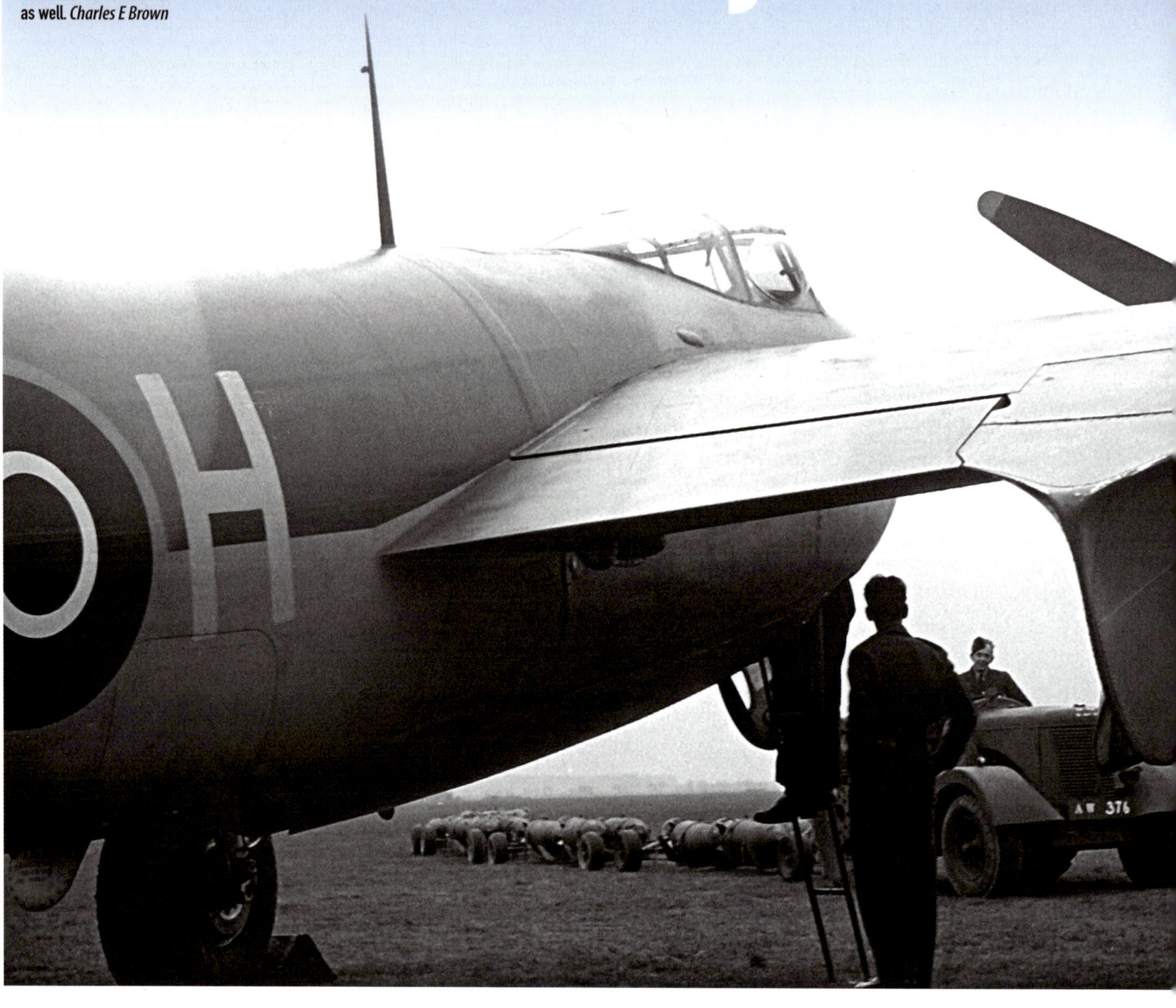

The Bomber

THE B.IV – After beginning official flight trials from February 1941, the prototype Mosquito B.IV, W4057 prototype was in the air by September. Nine B.IV Series 1s followed (W4064-W4072) all of which were completed by February 1942 and a further 300 B.IV Series 2 had left the Hatfield factory by September 1943.

The B.IV was the first 'light' bomber variant to enter squadron service, only differing from the original specification in carrying four 500lb bombs, twice the load that was originally planned. The Mosquito B.IV first entered RAF service with 2 (Light Bomber) Group, replacing the Blenheim which had been taking a pasting especially during low level daylight operations. 105 Squadron at Swanton Morley was to be the first recipient from November 1941. The squadron carried out its first operation, a daylight attack on Cologne, on May 31, 1942, the day after the city was struck by the first 'thousand-bomber' raid.

Mosquitoes flew operationally for 2 Group between May 1942 and May 1943, carrying out over 100 successful daylight raids with a much lower loss rate and considerably more clout than the Blenheim before it. By June 1942, 105 Squadron, which had by then moved to Marham, was joined by 139 (Jamaica) Squadron. One of 105 Squadron's raids that made the headlines was the daring attack on the Gestapo headquarters in Oslo on September 25, 1942. Operating at exceptionally low-level, 2 Group employed a 'low-level formation' and a 'shallow-diver formation' to achieve its goals. Both formations flew a co-ordinated attack. The 'shallow-divers' came in at 2,000ft and dropped their bombs at 1,500ft, while the 'low-levellers' came in straight at the target as low as possible.

105 Squadron were also the first Mosquito unit to bomb Berlin, striking the German capital on the morning of January 31, 1943. The attack was designed to disrupt a speech by Göring, which it duly did, and that afternoon 139 Squadron carried out a similar raid which also saw Goebbels running for cover during his speech.

Enter the B.IX

It was 109 Squadron at Wyton which was the first unit to receive the Mosquito B.IX from April 1943. The B.IX was powered by a pair of Merlin 72 engines, giving the aircraft an operational ceiling of 36,000ft. Capable of carrying the same four 500lb bombs in the bay as the B.IV, the B.IX could also carry two more under each wing. B.IXs serving with 8 Group were equipped with Oboe which was first used by 109 Squadron from Wyton during an attack on the Lutterade power station on the night of December 20/21, 1942.

From February 1944, modified versions of the B.IV, with a bulged bomb bay, became capable of carrying a single 4,000lb or 'cookie'. This modification was a standard feature of B.IXs.

The B.XVI & B.35 – The B.XVI, thanks to a pressurised cabin, was capable of operating at heights up to 40,000ft, way above normal interception height for the day. The combination of having the auxiliary tanks and its ability to carry a 4,000lb bomb, made the B.XVI ideal for raids on Berlin; a target that became the Mosquitoes speciality.

On March 12, 1945, the final British-built bomber variant, the B.35, made its maiden flight. An improved version of the B.XVI, the B.35 had a top speed of 422mph and could carry a 2,000lb bomb load for over 2,000 miles. The Second World War came to an end before the B.35 became operational, but the type still entered service with 109 and 139 Squadrons during the post-war years. These final Mosquito bombers were replaced by the Canberra during 1952 and 1953.

B.IV – An unarmed bomber as per the PR.1 with longer engine nacelles apart from the first nine that were built. Capable of carrying four 500lbs (short vaned), later increased to 4,000lb with the addition of a bulged bomb bay doors.
A/c: (Series 1) W4057, W4064-W4072; (Series 2) DK284-DK339, DZ311-DZ320, DZ340-DZ388, DZ404-DZ442, DZ458-DZ497, DZ515-DZ559, DZ575-DZ618 and DZ630-DZ652

B.V – Development of the B.IV, with a new 'standard wing' capable of carrying a pair of 50 gallon jettisonable fuel tanks or a pair of 500lb bombs. Prototype for the Canadian-built B.VII.

B.VII – The first batch of Canadian-built Mosquitoes were B.VIIs, based on the B.V and powered by the Merlin 31 engine. First flight from Toronto on September 24, 1942.
A/c: KB300-KB324

B.IX – High-altitude unarmed bomber, without a pressurised cabin, powered by a pair of Merlin 72 engines. Capable of carrying four 500lb bombs in the bay and two more under each wing.
A/c: LR475-LR477, LR495-LR513, ML896-ML924, MM237-MM238 and MM241

B.XVI – A per the B.IX but with a pressurized cabin and powered by the Merlin 72,73, 76 or 77 engines. Capable of carrying 3,000lbs of bombs but by 1944 all were converted to carry 4,000lb. 529 built.
A/c: ML925-ML942, ML956-ML999, MM112-MM156, MM169-MM205, MM219-MM226, PF379-PF415, PF428-PF469, PF481-PF526, PF538-PF579, PF592-PF619, RV295-RV326, RV340-RV347 and RV351-RV363

B.XX – As per the B.VII but furnished with Canadian/American equipment and powered by Packard Merlin 31 or 33 engines. The first two aircraft (KB162 and KB328) were delivered to Britain via Greenland in August 1943 and by

TECHNICAL SPECIFICATIONS B.IV

POWERPLANT:	Two 1,250hp Rolls-Royce Merlin 21 and 23
DIMENSIONS:	Span, 54ft 2in; length, 40ft 9½in; height, 15ft 3in; wing area, 454 sq ft
WEIGHTS:	Empty, 14,600lb; loaded 20,870lb
PERFORMANCE:	Max speed, 380mph at 17,000ft; climb, 22.5 min to 28,800ft; range 2,040 miles; service ceiling, 28,000ft
ARMAMENT:	Bomb load, 2,000lb later modified to carry 4,000lb 'Cookie'

Several B.IVs that were still in service were converted to carry a single 4,000lb what by fitting bulged bomb-bays. This is DZ594 during trials with the A&AEE; the aircraft later joined 627 Squadron before being SOC on June 28, 1945. *Via Martyn Chorlton*

late November were operational. The first B.XX operation was flown by 139 Squadron when KB161 bombed Berlin on December 2, 1943.

40 B.XXs were modified with aerial cameras, delivered to the USAAF and redesignated as the F.8 for meteorological and reconnaissance duties. A/c: KB100-KB299 and KB325-KB369.

B.23 – Development of the B.XX powered by Merlin 69 engines instead of the Merlin 255 in case supplies should run low. This never happened and the idea was abandoned.

B.25 – As per the Canadian-built B.XX but powered by Merlin 225 engines. A/c: KA930-KA999 and KB370-KB699

B.35 – Basically a B.XVI, but powered by Merlin 114 engines in the early production aircraft and Merlin 114A in the later. A/c: RS699-RS723, RV364-RV367, TA617-TA618, TA633-TA670, TA685-TA724, TH977-TH999, TJ113-TJ158, TK591-TK635, TK648-TK656, VP178-VP202 and VR792-VR806

The Fighter Bombers
THE UBIQUITOUS FB.VI

The most significant development of the NF.II was the FB.VI which, as a fighter bomber, was destined to become the most used Mosquito fighter of all. The prototype FB.VI, HJ662 first flew on June 1, 1942 but, while nearing the end of successful flight trials with the AAEE at Boscombe Down, an engine cut on take-off and the fighter was wrecked after hitting a pair of Beaufighters on the ground.

The first 300 FB.VIs built were dedicated fighter bombers and were given the additional designation Series 1. These were designed to

TECHNICAL SPECIFICATIONS FB.VI

POWERPLANT:	Two 1,230hp Rolls-Royce Merlin 21 or 1,635hp Merlin 25
DIMENSIONS:	Span, 54ft 2in; length, 40ft 6in; height, 12ft 6in; wing area, 435 sq ft
WEIGHTS:	Empty, 14,300lb; loaded 22,300lb
PERFORMANCE:	Max speed, 380mph at 13,000ft; climb, 7 min to 15,000ft; range 1,205 miles or 1,705 miles with underwing tanks; service ceiling, 33,000ft
ARMAMENT:	(Series 2) Four 20mm guns and four .303in guns forward and two 500lb bombs in fuselage and two 500lb bombs or eight RPs under the wings

carry a pair of 250lb bombs at the rear of the bomb-bay and one under each wing, as well as retaining four .303in machine guns and four 20mm cannon in the nose. The Series 2 went one stage further by raising the armament to a pair of 500lb bombs in the rear bomb-bay and two more under each wing; the standard nose armament was retained.

The FB.VI entered Fighter Command service in the role of day and night intruder and would later become a specialist at Ranger and Instep patrols. The Mosquito took over from the Boston III as an intruder, first joining 418 Squadron at Ford in May 1943. From December, the FB.VI was also serving Coastal Command, progressively replacing the Beaufighter in the anti-shipping role and becoming a particularly useful platform for

delivering unguided rocket projectiles (RP). The latter were first tested by FB.VI, HJ719 at Boscombe Down, in early 1943.

The FB.VI was very successful in the anti-shipping role, achieving notoriety with the Banff Strike Wing for despatching enemy shipping along the Norwegian coast from September 1944 through to the end of the Second World War. Armed with eight 60lb RPs

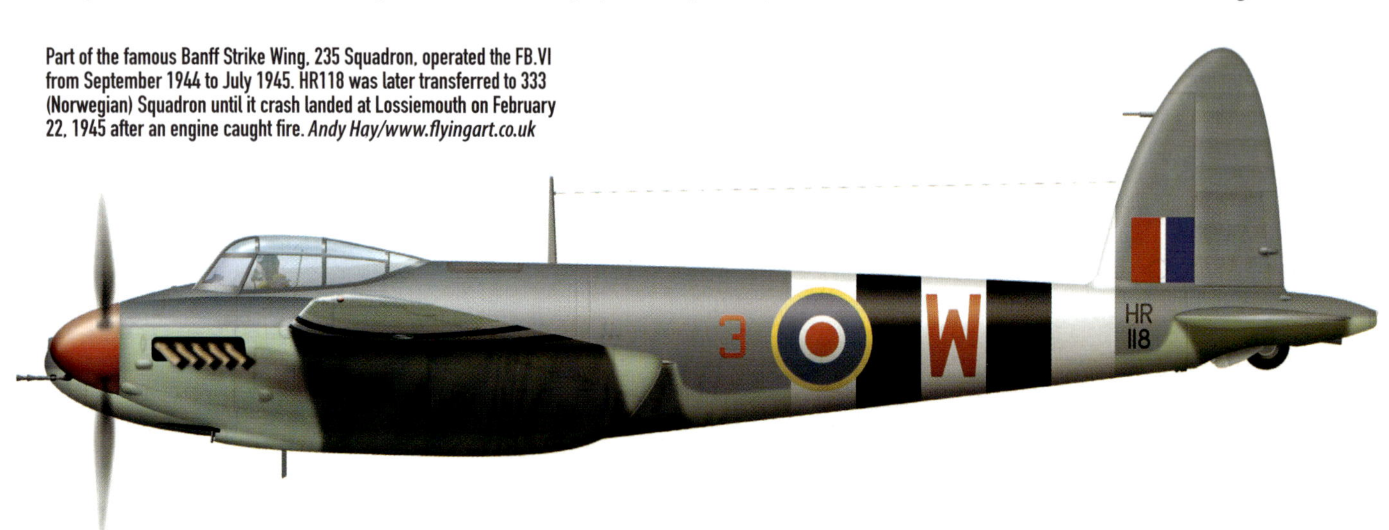

Part of the famous Banff Strike Wing, 235 Squadron, operated the FB.VI from September 1944 to July 1945. HR118 was later transferred to 333 (Norwegian) Squadron until it crash landed at Lossiemouth on February 22, 1945 after an engine caught fire. *Andy Hay/www.flyingart.co.uk*

529 Mosquito B.XVIs were built, a variant that cruised back and forth to Berlin almost unmolested from early 1944 through to the end of the Second World War. *Via Martyn Chorlton*

248 Squadron converted from the Beaufighter X to the Mosquito FB.VI in June 1943, which was joined by the FB.XVIII in January 1944. At the time of D-Day landings, when this shot was taken, this aircraft, NT225 was operating from Portreath. *Via Martyn Chorlton*

The sole FB.42, A52-500 was actually British-built ex-FB.II HR302 converted to Merlin 69 power. *Via Martyn Chorlton*

plus the standard nose guns, the firepower of the FB.VI was estimated to be the same as a broadside from a 10,000 ton cruiser! Another novel version, the FB.XVIII, was fitted with a 57mm Molins gun in the nose, the prototype, HJ732, first flew on June 8, 1943. Less than 20 were built, all of them joining 248 Squadron from October 1943.

Record upon record against the enemy

The Mosquito FB.VI also saw extensive service with the RAF's home defence night fighter squadrons, as well as continuing to intrude deep over Germany. A 605 Squadron crew achieved the type's 100th enemy victory over Fassberg on December 24, 1943. As if to demonstrate the unit's wide area of operations, 605 Squadron achieved its 101st victory over London on January 10/11, 1944 when a Ju188 was brought down in Germany's 'Little Blitz'.

605 Squadron continued to build on their previous records by shooting down the first enemy aircraft after 'H-hour' on June 6, 1944. A 25 Squadron FB.VI crew could claim the first enemy aircraft on D-Day itself when they brought down a Ju188 just after midnight.

A Mosquito FB.VI, flown by Flt Lt J G Musgrave, shot down the first of many V-1s over the English Channel on June 14/15, 1944 and, incredibly, by July 15, Mosquitoes of Fighter Command had shot 428. Of the latter tally, 96 Squadron claimed 181 of them and 605 Squadron 75.

Fighter-Bomber variants

FB.VI – A development of the NF.II with the same armament and an additional pair of 50 gallon wing tanks or two 500lb bombs. From 1944, aircraft were modified to carry four 60lb RPs under each wing instead of wing tanks.
A/c: HJ662-HJ682, HJ716-HJ743, HJ755-HJ792, HJ808-HJ833, HP848-HP888, HP904-HP942, HP967-HP989, HR113-HR220, HR236-HR262, HR279-HR312, HR331-HR375, HR387-HR415, HR432-HR465, HR485-HR527, HR539-HR580, HR603-HR649, HX802-HX835, HX849-HX869, HX896-HX901, HX905-HX922, HX937-HX984, LR248-LR276, LR289-LR313, LR327-LR340, LR343-LR389, LR402-LR404

FB.X – Merlin 67 powered version of the FB.VI. Not built.

FB.XVIII – A development of the FB.VI with a modified nose to accommodate a 6lb (57mm) Molins anti-tank gun in place of the standard four 20mm cannon arrangement. 20 built.
A/c: HJ732, HX902-HX904, MM424, MM425, PZ251, PZ252, PZ300, PZ301, PZ346 and PZ467-PZ470

FB.21 – As per a de Havilland-built FB.VI of which only three were built. Two were powered by Packard Merlin 31 engines and the other two by Merlin 33s.
A/c: KA100-KA102

FB.24 – High-altitude development of the FB.21 powered by two-stage, supercharged Merlin 301 engines. Only one built.

FB.26 – Another development of the FB.VI this time powered by Merlin 225 engines and furnished with Canadian/American equipment. Designed to replace the FB.21, 398 FB.26s were built.
A/c: KA103-KA119, KA123-KA136, KA140, KA142-KA148, KA151-KA157, KA159-KA165, KA168-KA171, KA175-KA201, KA204, KA205, KA208-KA220, KA222-KA231, KA235-KA241, KA244-KA279, KA282-KA289, KA291-KA296, KA302-KA311, KA315-KA540

FB.28 – Planned successor to the FB.26 powered by Merlin 25 engines. Not built.

FB.40 – Australian-built version of the FB.VI fitted with de Havilland hydromatic or Hamilton Standard propellers. The first FB.40 flew from Sydney on July 23, 1943. 178 FB.40s were built, the first 100 powered by Merlin 31 engines and the remainder by Merlin 33s.
A/c: A52-1 to A52-212

FB.42 – A single aircraft, ex-FB.40, was modified with Merlin 69 engines but the idea was shelved and the Mosquito became the prototype PR.41.
A/c: A52-36

Armed with eight 60lb RPs, plus the standard nose guns, the firepower of the FB.VI could pack quite a punch. *Aeroplane*

One week's Mosquito production by the Percival Aircraft Company parked on the grass at Luton in early 1945. The ten Mosquitoes are all B.XVIs. Percival built 195 B.XVIs between May 1944 and December 1945 and 50 PR.34s between September 1945 and July 1946.
Charles E Brown via Aeroplane

This well-known photo shows a line-up of Mosquito B.IVs of 105 Squadron at RAF Marham, Norfolk in December 1942. The squadron was the subject of this article by *The Aeroplane*. Aeroplane

Mosquito In the Day Offensive

The Aeroplane, January 15, 1943 by P.F.M.

EXPRESS DELIVERY — A de Havilland Mosquito in the background awaits its load of four 500-lb. bombs to be carried in daylight to Germany at a higher speed than in any other bomber in the World. *Aeroplane*

High performance bomber

BOMBER COMMAND is now using de Havilland Mosquito bombers for low level attacks on targets in Western Europe. Manned by picked air crews, these bombers have been taking part during the past two months in the offensive of Fighter, Bomber and Army Co-operation Commands, particularly against the transport and communications systems under the control of the Germans.

Only very small numbers of Mosquitoes have failed to return from operations on the other side of the English Channel and North Sea. The defensive characteristics required by Mosquitoes to protect themselves from the cannon and machine-gun fire of the Focke-Wulf and Messerschmitt fighters of the Luftwaffe lie in the aerodynamic efficiency and sound workmanship of the aeroplane, which closely follows the almost perfect aerodynamic form of the de Havilland Albatross, combined with the immense power compressed into the two Rolls-Royce Merlin 21 motors.

Military specifications must always include some items which will break the clean lines of a prototype or civil aeroplane. In the Mosquito the nose has had to be flattened to allow the Observer to use the bomb sight when operating at high levels for precision bombing. This, with one or two other imperfections, has made the performance of the operational Mosquito slightly lower than that of a possible civil mail-carrying version, but even so. The top speed of the Mosquito at 'deck' level is exceptional.

The performance of the Mosquito does not end with its high speed, but also includes a very fast rate of climb and a range which is long enough to enable squadrons equipped with Mosquitoes to operate over Norway and far inside Germany itself. This range is combined with a high cruising speed well above that of any other bomb-carrying aeroplane.

When one Mosquito was attacked by a Focke-Wulf Fw 190A3 it went into so tight a turn that the Fw 190 with its wider turning radius was unable to get the bomber in its gun sight.

At low levels the performance of the Mosquito is excellent. The squadrons have, therefore, been trained in the new methods of low level, hedge hopping attacks and now the de Havilland Mosquito is being used in conjunction with the Mustangs, Spitfires and Bostons of Army Co-operation and Fighter Commands in their combined attacks on Western Europe.

Attacks are often made either at dusk, after approaching a target in daylight to return in the dark, or at dawn after setting out in the early hours of the morning to return in time for breakfast, although some raids are made in the hours of broad daylight.

Precision bomber squadron

One Mosquito Squadron* is commanded by Wing Commander H. I. Edwards, V.C., D.S.O., D.F.C., who has 53 operational sorties to his credit, and includes Squadron Leader D. A. G Parry, D.S.O., D.F.C., who led the. raid on the Nazi Party Headquarters at Oslo, Squadron Leader J. R. G. Ralston, D.S.O., D.F.M., hero of 74 sorties, including the unique operation of blocking a railway tunnel in France at both ends while a train was inside, and Flight Lieutenant S. C. Clayton, D.F.C., D.F.M., who has been on more operational flights than any other Observer in Bomber Command

105 Squadron was the first RAF unit to operate the Mosquito B.IV which it first received at Swanton Morely, Norfolk in November 1941. The squadron remained a Mosquito unit until it was disbanded at Upwood, by then operating the Mosquito B.XVI, in February 1946. *Aeroplane*

Sqn Ldr D A G 'George' Parry, DSO, DFC (right) with his observer, Fg Off 'Robbie' Robson in front of their personal aircraft, B.IV DK296 'G' for George. It was in this aircraft that Parry led the successful attack on the Gestapo HQ in Oslo. *Aeroplane* ▼

(he only wants another seven to complete his century).

The crews gather together in the crew room. Aircraft recognition charts, supplemented with numbers of solid models hung from the ceiling, provide a constant reminder of the possibilities of meeting enemy aircraft. Instructions in the form of charts cover the walls and include the procedure to be adopted when baling out. Both motors have to be stopped because the airscrew's arc approaches near to the escape and entrance

B.IV DZ360 'A' of 105 Squadron photographed just off the concrete apron in from of Marham's large 'C' Type hangars. Only days after The Aeroplane's visit, the bomber was shot down by a hail of light flak during an attack on Termonde; Flt Sgt J S Cloutier RCAF and Sgt A C Foxley were killed. *Aeroplane*

hatch in the floor of the cockpit.

The charts detail dinghy procedure in case a Mosquito has to alight on the sea and give information about the Air-Sea rescue service. All members of the air crews of Mosquito carry a whistle attached to the right lapel of their battle dress blouses as a substitute for shouting to attract attention.

There are notes on the ill effects of cold and height on the fighting qualities of air crews, a diagram of the flare path system in use on the home aerodromes, drawings of ships both, Allied and enemy, the new phonetic alphabet which has been adopted by the R.A..F. for radio telephony, information on the handling of D.H. airscrews, and a drawing of the oxygen economiser system.

Other charts of a more highly secret nature give information about the controls and coolant systems of the Mosquito, and yet another gives hints on how to obtain the best operational performance. Apparatus is provided for testing flying helmets before leaving the crew room. A lighter side which takes the pilots' minds away from the ever present reminders of war is provided by the constantly used radio set, a chess board, and numbers of topical magazines which lie on the large table in the centre of the room.

On a sortie, the two members of the Mosquito's crew are accommodated in the forward part of the fuselage. The rear part, which contains the oxygen, radio, and recognition lights as well as a large amount of other fixed equipment, is sealed before take-off and no entry to it is possible in flight. The pilot sits on the left of the cockpit with his observer on his right. A prone position on the right-hand side of the nose is left for the use of the Observer, but it is only used for high level precision bombing. All navigation up to within

seven or eight miles of a target is the duty of the Observer who also operates the two-way radio while keeping a look-out at the back of the machine for hostile fighters. When Mosquitoes operate in pairs or larger formations, all the navigation is done by the Observer in the leading aeroplane while the Observers in other machines watch for enemy aircraft.

Once aboard the air crews settle down in their places, check all the equipment, rev. up the motors, close the bomb doors, operated by a hydraulic system (as is the undercarriage), on four 500-lb. bombs and prepare to take off.

Then with main and tail wheels retracted the Mosquitoes swiftly climb and streak across the English countryside. Over the sea they go down to a slightly lower level before making a landfall. This landfall is said to be one of the most important parts of a sortie. If an aeroplane can fly straight over the coast up to its target it will strike with all the advantages of surprise on its side. But if an aeroplane flies on to its target after flying up and down the coast trying to find the correct landmark, it will arrive to find a hot reception prepared for it. As only one bombing run is made, landmarks are followed right up to the target. Five or six miles before it, the pilot takes over the navigation, opens the bomb doors, and advances the throttle. Then, going in at 'nought' feet, the Mosquitoes flash over their targets dropping all their bombs. These bombs are fitted with delayed-action fuses to enable the aeroplane to get anything up to a mile away before they explode.

When marshalling yards are being attacked the bombs often hit hard surfaces and because they are dropped so low at high speed, they strike with glancing blows. As a result they often bounce or ricochet sometimes even higher the aeroplanes which

dropped them, to go off eventually in some place where they will succeed in helping to cripple the German War effort.

On the run up to the target, Mosquitoes may attack in formation. After bombing, the machines break formation and race for home.

Amiens and Tergnier

Two typical dusk attacks took place on January 3**, when small formations of Mosquitoes attacked marshalling yards in Northern France. They gave an opportunity for the Royal Air Force to demonstrate the destructive power of its light day bomber squadrons.

Thorough preparations were made before the raid. The crews learnt by heart the contours of the ground around their targets and in the late afternoon six Mosquitoes took off to raid marshalling yards. When a mile away from the target, light anti-aircraft fire engaged the raiders, flying in echelon to starboard with their bomb doors open. None of the machines was hit, and they still escaped undamaged when some heavy anti-aircraft batteries opened up with short-fused shells. These burst above the aeroplanes and were completely ineffective.

Running straight on to the target, all our aircraft dropped their bombs and wrecked rolling stock, the rolling-stock repair shop and engine sheds. After closing their bomb doors the Mosquitoes returned without loss, in formation, to their aerodromes somewhere in England.

While this raid was taking place, more Mosquitoes were attacking another marshalling yard. After making successful landfall on the French coast, the aeroplanes flew across country low enough to let one pilot bring back to this country some of France's brushwood. All of the bombs

DZ353 and DZ367, in close company, over the Norfolk countryside in December 1942. *Aeroplane*

landed in the target area and one of the pilots insists that no trains left the target area that night.

One pilot recently had a running fight with a Focke-Wulf Fw 190 which lasted for more than 20 minutes. At first the Mosquito tried to shake off the Fw 190 by going round in tight turns, but his opponent followed. Seeing that the position was not at all favourable at the height at which they were flying, the crew of the Mosquito brought their machine down to ground level, taking evasive action all the time. Low down the Mosquito was able to show its heels to the Fw 190, which was mainly concerned with avoiding the trees which persisted in getting in the way. The German pilot was so concerned with the trees that he let the Mosquito escape after having fired only two bursts, both of which went wide.

On another occasion, the same Mosquito was attacked by a Messerschmitt Me 110. This time the speed and climb of the British aeroplane enabled it to slip up into a convenient cloud, completely baffling the slower Messerschmitt.

During the hours of daylight pilots have observed many of the population in Holland and the other occupied territories standing in the open waving to our aircraft. On the other hand, Germans usually dive for cover at the approach of any British aeroplanes. At night, the friendly attitude of the Dutch population can be judged from the numbers of 'Vs' which are incessantly flashed into the air from torches and windows. One of our pilots flew across Holland one night flashing the letter 'V' from his recognition lamp and he found the sign flashed back all along his route.

Norway raids

From conversations with Squadron Leader Parry and other members of the air crews who took part in the raids on Oslo***, we gather that the Nazis on that day had flown many of their latest aeroplanes to Kjeller aerodrome, near Oslo, to present a flying exhibition, which they hoped would bolster up the morale of their troops and impress the Norwegian population. When our four Mosquitoes arrived over Oslo, two Fw 190s were already in the air. Our pilots were extremely surprised to find such aeroplanes there but even more surprised were the Fw 190 pilots to find such high-speed bombers operating over Norway.

The Mosquitoes were flying in line astern and both Fw 190s attacked the rear machine, which was last seen going down with clouds of thick black smoke coming from one motor.

◄ Armourers hard at work preparing for the day's bombing raid from Marham. At this time, 105 Squadron was under the command of VC winner, Wg Cdr (later Air Cdre) H I Edwards who had been in charge since May 1941. *Aeroplane*

◄ Four bombs are detached from the 'bomb train' on their own trolley for each aircraft and then hand cranked into the Mosquitoes, bomb-bay by the armourers. *Aeroplane*

Dramatic attack photograph taken from Sqn Ldr Parry's Mosquito during the attack on the Gestapo HQ in Oslo on September 25, 1942. The photograph has been annotated; (A) debris and smoke begins to rise after a direct hit; (B) a central cupola above the Nazi HQ from which a Swastika flag could be seen flying and (C) Oslo University, completely undamaged in the pin-point raid. *Via Martyn Chorlton* ➤

Nothing was seen of the Fw 190s after that for a second or two until the Observer in the third Mosquito saw cannon and machine-gun fire going past just above his head. By that time, the bomb doors had been closed and our aeroplanes were able to fly out to sea, out-distancing the two German fighters who made a futile attempt to catch the Mosquitoes by chasing them for some 60 miles or so.

Only at one point in the whole operation were the Mosquitoes open to attack; that was when their bomb doors were open. Luck was with the Focke-Wulfs; otherwise they could never have taken off and intercepted the Mosquitoes, which succeeded, all the same, in wrecking the three small buildings that constituted the Nazi Party Headquarters in Oslo. The way in which these three buildings were identified among the many similar buildings in the town of Oslo was a notable feat in itself and exemplifies the best tactical use of the Mosquito against spot targets. Night bombers can rain an enormous weight of bombs on large areas but no night bomber can single out small targets, each of which has to be destroyed with the least amount of damage to surrounding, possibly civilian, property and with the smallest possible waste of high explosive.

The Mosquito's wood construction has proved as adequate to its task as any metal airframe. Fire does not appear to be causing any trouble and although one or two fires have been known to occur as a result of short circuiting after radio sets have been damaged, they have not spread and many of them have been put out by the Observers while still in flight. The wood stands up to cannon and machine-gun fire.

Manned by some of the most famous and competent aircrews in the world, the de Havilland Mosquito light bomber squadrons of Bomber Command will continue to take advantage of every opportunity offered them to strike deep and hard into the resources of the Reich. ✤

* 105 Squadron
** The operation on January 3, 1943 was carried out by six Mosquito B.IVs of 105 Squadron against railway targets in the Amiens and Tergnier areas; all returned safely back to Marham.
*** The raid on the Oslo Gestapo HQ took place on September 25, 1942; the four aircraft involved carrying out the attack from Leuchars. The one aircraft lost was B.IV DK325 flown by Flt Sgt G K Carter and Sgt W S Young.

The operation involved a round trip of 1,100 miles which, at the time, was the longest Mosquito operation of the war.

Only days after this original article was published, the high risk strategy of attacking at low height in broad daylight claimed another victim on January 23, 1943. DZ311 was one of four Mosquitoes detailed to attack the Osnabrück railway yards. The aircraft was lost, and its pilot, Plt Off L J Skinner, and observer/navigator, Sgt F H Saunders, were killed. *Andy Hay/www.flyingart.co.uk*

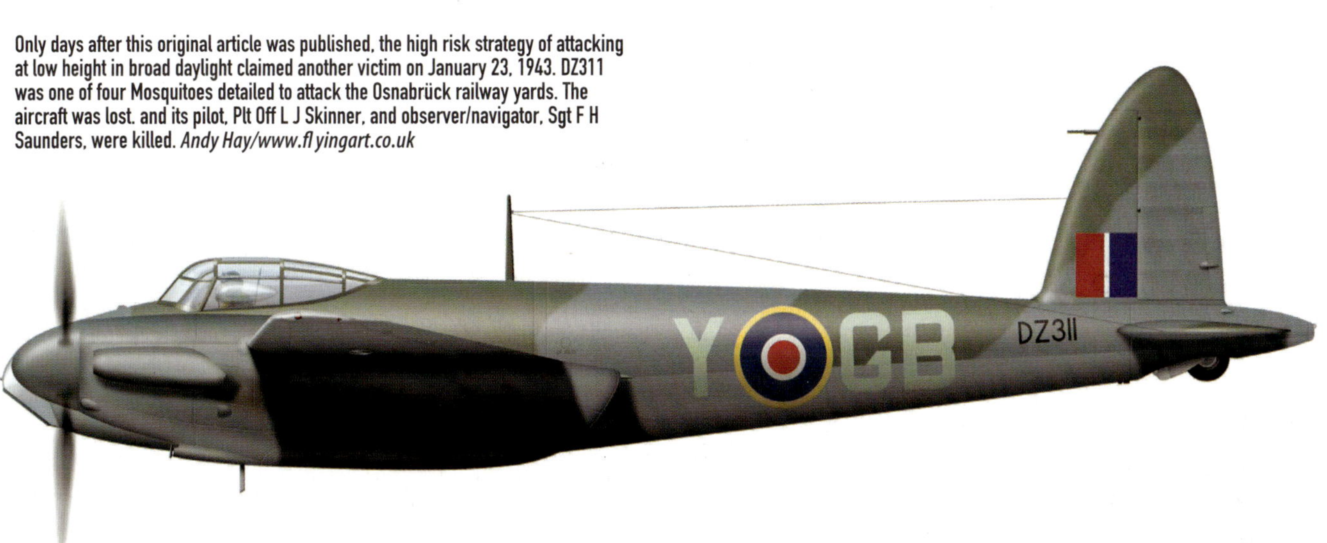

The De Havilland Mosquito IV

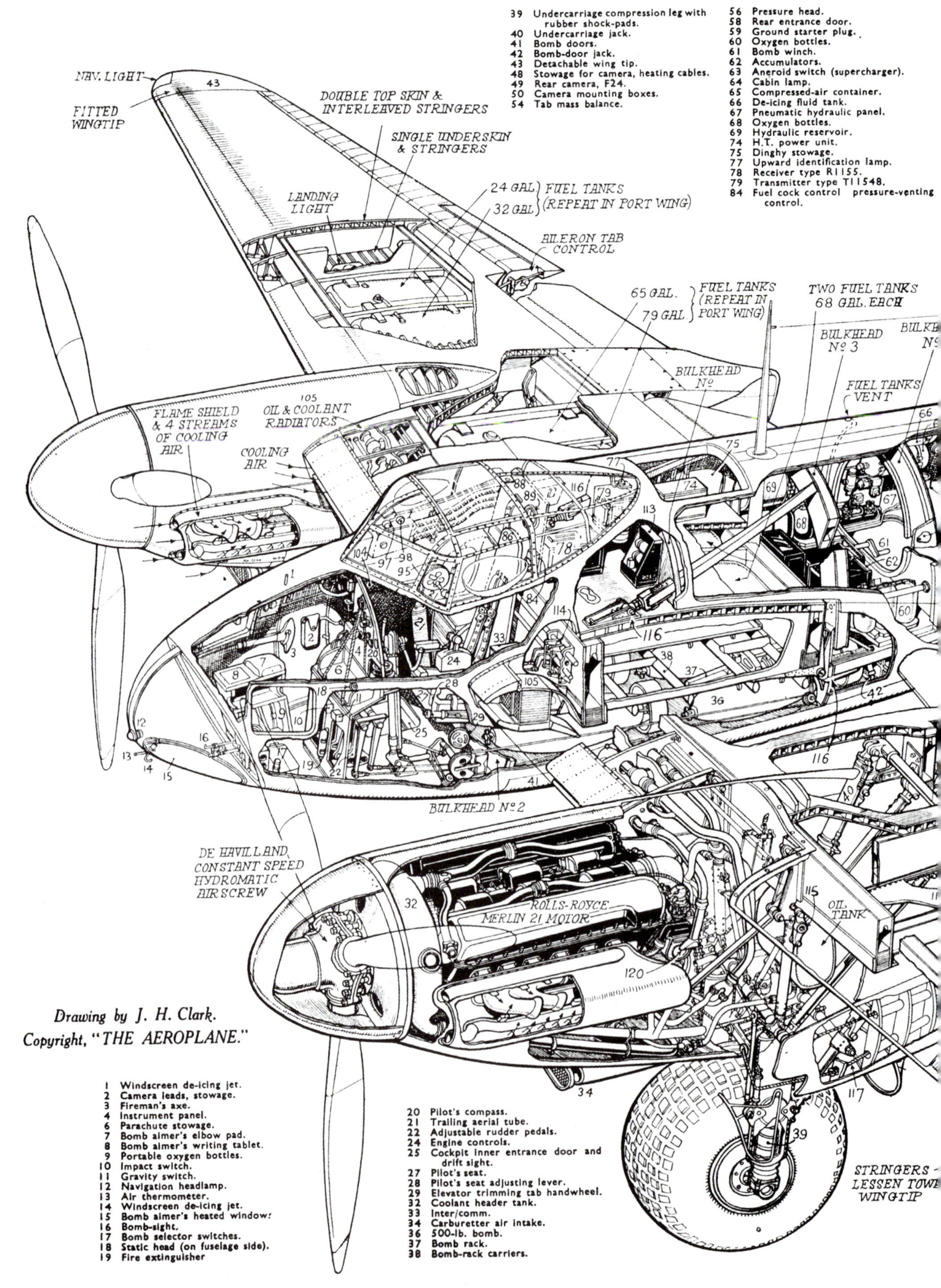

Drawing by J. H. Clark.
Copyright, "THE AEROPLANE."

86 Pilot's armour.
88 Observer's armour.
89 Observer's window.
95 Hinged window.
97 Signalling switch (formation keeping).
98 Signalling switch (identification).
104 Navigation table.
105 Oil and coolant radiators.
106 Fin fixings.
107 Rudder control spring-loaded rod.
108 Rudder mass balance
109 Rudder linkage.
110 Support rods for rear spar of tail-plane.
111 Elevator mass balance.
112 Operating jack for retracting tail-wheel.
113 Voltage regulator.
114 Throttle and airscrew control rods.
115 Lug for jacking undercarriage.
116 Wing fixing.
117 Elastic cable for undercarriage door.
118 Inspection doors to fuel tank bays.
119 Four longerons between ply skin.
120 Magneto heating.

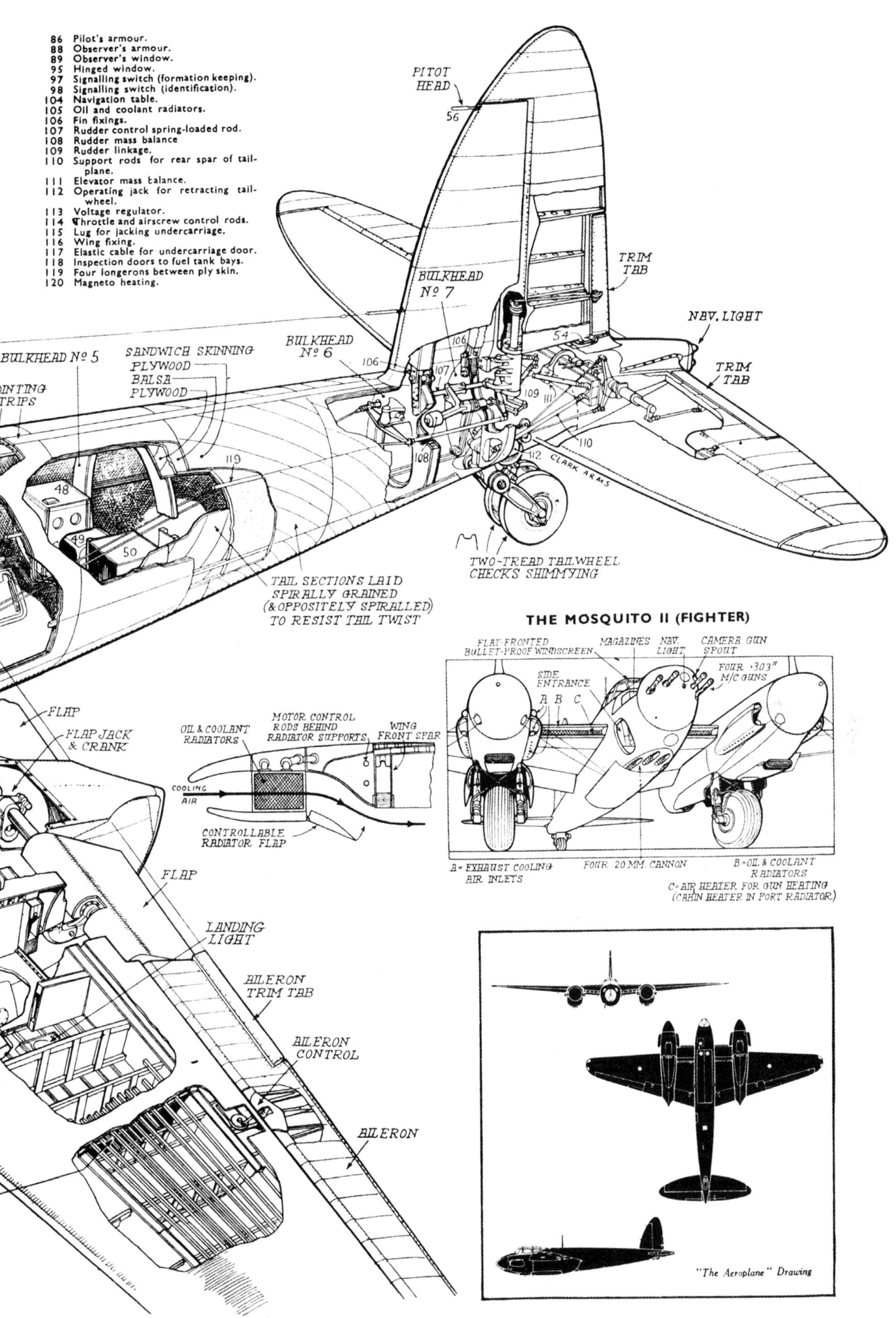

No place to hide

The Mosquito night fighter served the RAF for a decade, a role it was particularly suited to, with the type maturing at the same pace as the radar it carried. Owen Cooper describes the night fighter variants from the NF.II through to the NF.38, and highlights some of its operations.

A de Havilland Mosquito NF.II undertakes a night firing test of its four 20mm cannon and four .303in machine-guns. *Via author*

The prototype Mosquito NF.II W4052 (only the third aircraft built) which served as a trials and test bed throughout its flying career which ended on November 26, 1946. *Via author*

W4052 fitted with an experimental full circumference airbrake pictured in its fully extended position. *Via author*

Another modification applied to W4052 was the installation of a combined AI radar and Turbinlite searchlight in the nose. *Via author*

The first production NF.XII, HJ945 shows the fitment of just the four 20mm cannon under the fuselage to make room for the AI Mk VIII radar in the nose. *Via author*

Converted from the NF.II, the NF.XVII was the first Mosquito night–fighter to be fitted with the American AI Mk X radar. This is DZ659 which served solely with the FIU until it was SOC on February 28, 1946. *Via author*

The Merlin–25 powered NF.XIX first entered service with 257 Squadron in May 1944. MM652, pictured, joined 157 and then 169 Squadron before being sold by de Havilland to Sweden on October 27, 1948. *Via author*

Night defender

The Mosquito's versatility is the stuff of legend – as well as serving as a high speed long range light bomber, the aircraft was pressed into service as a tactical fighter-bomber firing machine guns, cannon and rocket projectiles (RPs), and became an effective and feared anti-shipping aircraft serving Coastal Command and, as described here, as a radar-equipped night fighter.

At home, the night fighter truly excelled and helped to defend Britain for some three years, claiming 600 enemy aircraft and more than 600 V-1 flying bombs shot down. The fighter-bombers wreaked havoc across German-occupied Europe, disrupting communications, wrecking supply lines, and regularly targeting enemy troop movements. Further afield in the Far East, the same activities were undertaken and, with Coastal Command, Mosquitoes armed with 20-mm cannon, RPs, and in a few cases with 6lb nose guns, helped to destroy, and damage thousands of tons of enemy shipping.

Modifying the contract

From the outset, interest from the Air Ministry, which originally ordered the Mosquito as a light bomber, quickly switched in favour of the fighter variant. Even by 1940, the original contract for 50 bombers had been modified to 30 fighters and 20 bombers. Externally, the fighter variant did not differ a great deal from the bomber but, under the skin, modifications included a much stronger main wing spar to help deal with the higher loads experienced during combat, while the nose was changed to accommodate four 20mm cannon and four .303in machine guns. The windscreen was also changed to a flat, later bullet-proof, type and access to the cockpit was changed from a floor hatch, as per the bomber, to a door on the starboard side of the fuselage.

The last of the three prototypes, W4052, was equipped as a night fighter to Air Ministry Specification F.21/40 and designated as the Mosquito NF.II. It first flew in this guise from a meadow behind Salisbury Hall on May 15, 1941. W4052 was fitted with the very latest radar equipment available, the AI Mk IV (though the AI Mk V was soon installed), which was specifically designed for intercepting enemy bombers at night. Its installation was characterised by a 'bow-and-arrow' aerial in the nose.

W4052 spent its entire career as a flying testbed for a host of night fighter tactical trials and equipment development work, serving only de Havilland, the A&AEE and the FIU over a five year period. Experiments included the fitment of a mock-up dorsal turret for three extra cannon and two types of bellows-operated airbrakes which opened and closed around the circumference of the mid-fuselage. W4052 was even, briefly, fitted with a Turbinlite searchlight in the nose before the long-serving prototype was SOC on November 26, 1946.

The first of 398 Mosquito NF.IIs built entered service with Fighter Command from January 1942, the type steadily replacing the Beaufighter and the Havoc. No 157 Squadron at Castle Camps was the first unit to receive the NF.II, followed by 23 Squadron at Ford and, on April 27/28, the first operational night sortie was flown. By the end of the year, 23 Squadron was moved to Luqa where, on December 30/31, the first night intruder operation over the Mediterranean was flown. Between January and March 1943, 23 Squadron shot down 17 enemy aircraft and also quickly became adept at shooting up trains in Italy, North Africa, and Sicily.

Better radar, better night fighter

New night fighter variants arrived in service at the same rate as radar development. The NF.XII joined the ranks in January 1943, with the British AI Mk VIII centimetric radar fitted. To accommodate the new radar a thimble radome was fitted, and the four .303in machine guns were removed from the nose leaving only the four cannon, which proved to be adequate armament for all subsequent night fighters.

Ninety seven NF.XIIs were converted from NF.II airframes, the first of them joining 85 Squadron at Hunsdon from February 1943 followed by 256 Squadron at Ford in May.

The NF.XIII was a new-build development equivalent to the NF.XII. This introduced the soon to be familiar 'bull' nose, accommodating the AI Mk VIII radar. The next night fighter variant, the NF.XVII, was converted from NF.IIs, it was very similar to the NF.XII but was the first of its kind to be fitted with the American AI Mk X (SCR-720) centimetric radar. Ninety nine NF.XVIIs were produced and the first of them joined 25 Squadron in December 1943. During a single sortie on March 19, 1944 Flt Lt Singleton and his navigator Flt Lt G Haslam in HK255 shot down three Ju188s, firmly endorsing 25 Squadron's new choice of aircraft.

The NF.XVII was superseded by the Merlin 25-powered NF.XIX which entered service in

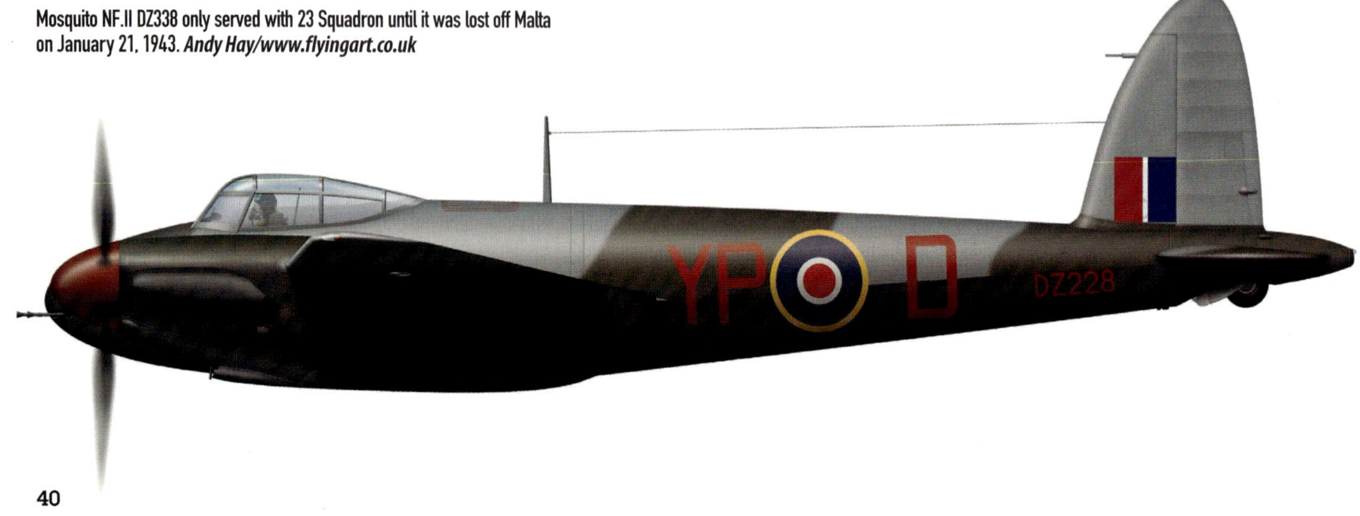

Mosquito NF.II DZ338 only served with 23 Squadron until it was lost off Malta on January 21, 1943. *Andy Hay/www.flyingart.co.uk*

The prototype NF.38 was the former NF36 RL248, pictured at Hatfield on January 22, 1947. The night fighter only served the manufacturers and the TFU before being retired in September 1954. *Via author* ⌄

530 Mosquito NF.XXXs (NF.30 post–war) were built, a large number of them seeing operational service during the later stages of the Second World War. RK953 served with 151 Squadron until it was SOC on August 21, 1950. *Via author*

May 1944 with 257 Squadron. This variant, of which 280 were built, had the ability to accommodate either British or American-built radar sets.

The last Mosquito night fighter variant to see operational service during World War Two was the NF.XXX (NF.30). Initially powered by the high-altitude rated Merlin 72, from the 31st NF.XXX built, these were replaced by the Merlin 76 and later with the 113 series engines. 526 of this mark were built, the vast majority at de Havilland's Leavesden plant. By May 1945, seven RAF squadrons tasked with home defence with 11 and 12 Group Fighter Command and a further three squadrons with 100 Group, were still in service.

Nocturnal 'Mossie', post-war

Two further night fighter marks were destined to see service with the post-war RAF, the first of them was the NF.36, the prototype, RK955, first flying in May 1945. A development of the NF.XXX, the NF.36 was powered by a pair of Merlin 113 engines and fitted with an American AI Mk X radar (with an unusual transparent radome) and four 20mm cannon. 163 NF.36s were built at Leavesden.

The very final night fighter variant and the last of all of the Mosquitoes to be built was the NF.38 which flew for the first time on November 18, 1947. Very similar to the NF.36, the only major difference was a British AI Mk IX radar. All 101 NF.38s were built either at Hatfield or Chester, the very last of them, VX916, left the Chester factory in November 1950; it was the last of 6,439 built in Britain and the last of 7,781, the total built, including Australian and Canadian production. ✤

TECHNICAL SPECIFICATIONS (all NF marks)

POWERPLANT: (II, XII, XIII) Two Rolls-Royce Merlin 21 and 23; (XIX) Two Merlin 25; (XXX) Two 1,690hp Merlin 72 (1st 70 a/c), 76 or 113/114; (36) Two Merlin 113; (38) Two Merlin 113/114 or 113A and 114A.

DIMENSIONS: (XXX) Span, 54ft 2in; length, 41ft 9in; height, 12ft 6in; wing area, 435sq ft

WEIGHTS: (XII) All-up, 18,720lb; (XIII) All-up, 21,000lb; (XV) All-up, 17,600lb; (XVII) 20,400lb; (XIX) All-up, 21,750lb; (XXX) Empty, 15,400lb; loaded 21,600lb; all-up 22,700lb

PERFORMANCE: (XII) Max speed, 394mph; (XXX) Max speed, 407mph at 28,000ft; climb, 7½ min to 15,000ft; range 1,300 miles or 1,770 miles with underwing tanks; service ceiling, 39,000ft

ARMAMENT: (II) Four 20mm cannon and four .303in machine guns; (XII, XXX, 36) Four 20mm cannon.

TANKAGE *(max fuel load possible with LR tanks/fuel with max useful load in gallons):* (II) 547/453; (XII) 507/403; (XIII) 716/453; (XV) 335/335; (XVII) 547/403; (XIX) 716/453

RADAR: (II) AI Mk IV and V; (XII & XIII) AI Mk VIII; (XVII & 36) American AI Mk X; (XIX) AI Mk VIII or AI Mk X; (38) AI Mk IX.

PRODUCTION (DOES NOT INCLUDED CONVERSIONS)

NF.II (398) A/c: W4052 (Prototype), W4073-W4099, DD600-DD644, DD659-DD691, DD712-DD759, DD777-DD800, DZ228-DZ272, DZ286-DZ310, DZ653-DZ661, DZ680-DZ727, DZ739-DZ761, HJ642-HJ661, HJ699-HJ715 & HJ911-HJ944

NF.XII (97 NF.IIs converted) A/c: HJ945, HJ946, HK107-HK141 & HK159-HK235

NF.XIII (270) A/c: HK363-HK382, HK396-HK437, HK453-HK481, HK499-HK536, MM436-MM479, MM491-MM534, MM547-MM590, MM615-MM623, SM700 & SM702 (re-serialled from HK535 & HK536)

NF.XIV A high altitude variant of the NF.XIV with Merlin 67 engines. Not built

NF.XV (5) A/c: DZ342, DZ364, DZ385, DZ404 & DZ424

NF.XVII (99) A/c: DZ659, HK236-HK265, HK278-HK327 & HK344-HK362.

NF.XIX (280) A/c: MM624-MM656, MM669-MM685, TA123-TA198, TA215-TA249, TA263-TA308, TA323-TA357, TA389-TA413 & TA425-TA449

NF.30 (530) A/c: MM686-MM710, MM726-MM769, MM783-MM822, MT456-MT500, MV521-MV570, NT241-NT283, NT295-NT336, NT349-NT393, NT415-NT458, NT471-NT513, NT526-NT568, NT582-NT621 and RK929-RK954

NF.31 Packard Merlin NF variant that never left the drawing board

NF.36 (163) A/c: RK955-RK960, RK972-RK999, RL113-RL158, RL173-RL215 and RL229-RL268

NF.38 (101) A/c: RL248, VT651-VT683, VT691-VT707, VX860-VX879 & VX886-VX916

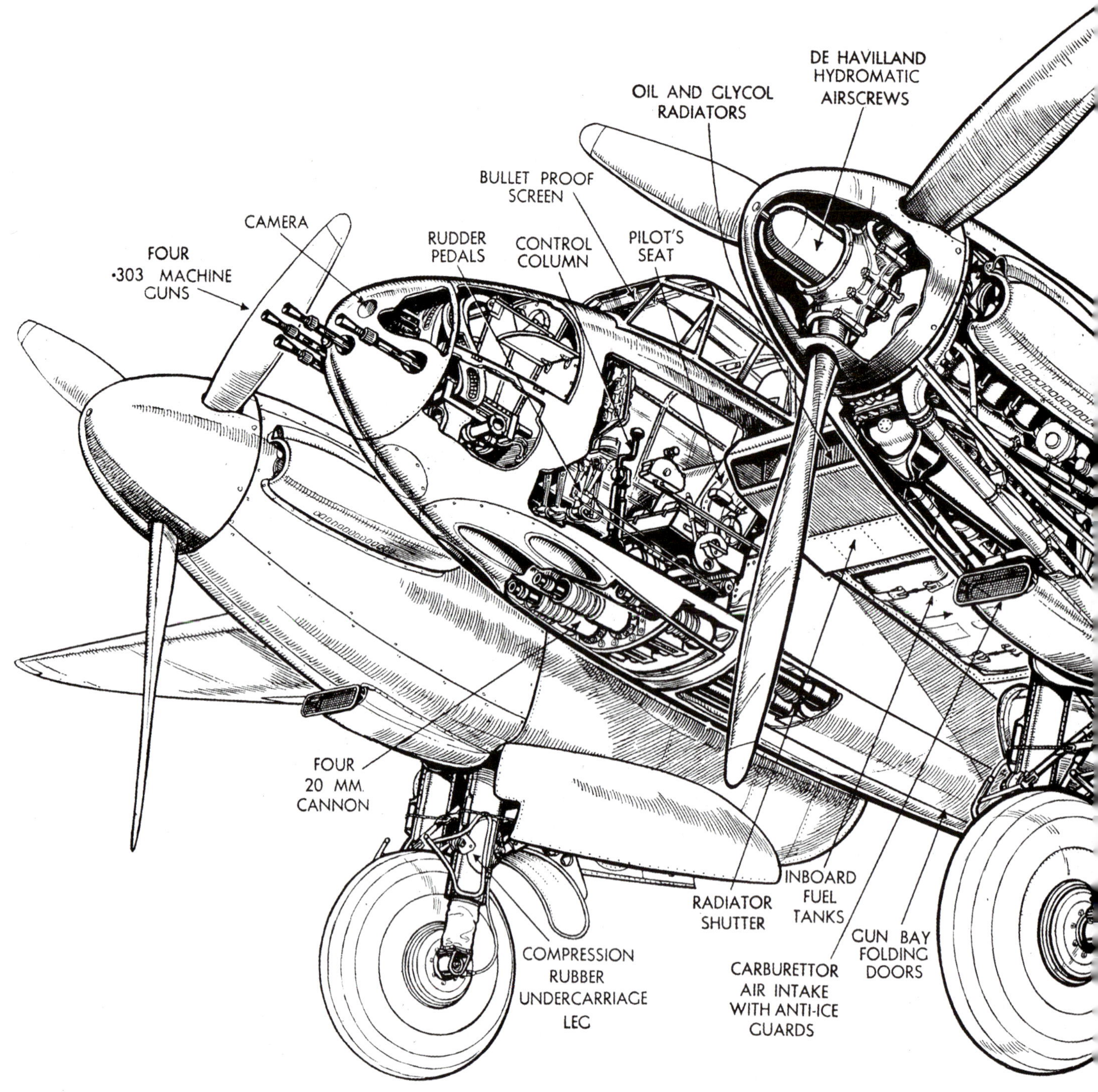

In this copyright drawing by our chief artist, Mr. M. A. Millar, the general layout of the Mosquito is clearly revealed. The primary structure is of wood, largely in the form of plywood. Other constructional details will be found on the preceding pages. Notable features are the leading-edge radiators and the use of compression rubber blocks in the undercarriage legs. The crew of two comprises pilot and navigator, who are seated side by side. The machine guns and cannon are fired electro-pneumatically by switches on the control column. The guns and cabin are heated by air from the radiators.

DATA

Two Merlin XXI Engines

Duty : Two-seater long-range fighter	Aspect ratio	7
Crew (2) : Pilot and observer	Max. fuselage depth	5ft. 5.5in.
	Max. fuselage width	4ft. 5in.
Length o.a.	41ft. 2in.	Wheel track — 16ft. 4in.
Wing span	54ft. 2in.	
Wing area (gross)	436 sq. ft.	Normal loaded weight — 18,540 lb.
Root chord	12ft. 3in.	Wing loading — 42.5 lb./sq. ft.
Tip chord	3ft. 10in.	Power loading — 7.4 lb./h.p.

The Rolls-Royce Merlin XXI Engine

Bore	5.4in.	Capacity	1,649 cu. in. (27 litres)
Stroke	6.0in.	Max. power	1,250 b.h.p.

De Havilland Mosquito F.II (Fighter)

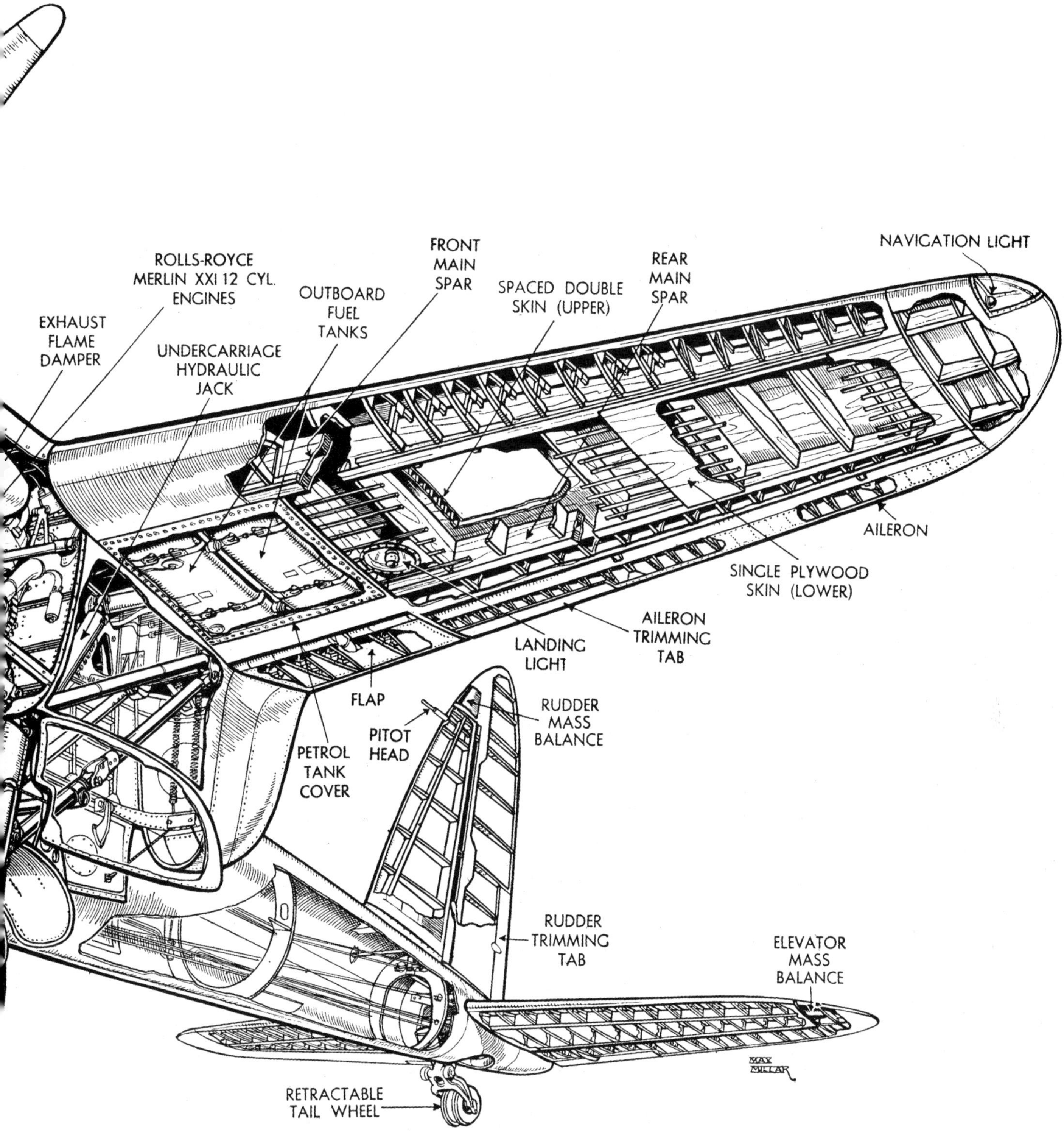

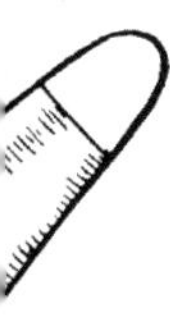

EXHAUST
FLAME
DAMPER

ROLLS-ROYCE
MERLIN XXI 12 CYL.
ENGINES

UNDERCARRIAGE
HYDRAULIC
JACK

OUTBOARD
FUEL
TANKS

FRONT
MAIN
SPAR

SPACED DOUBLE
SKIN (UPPER)

REAR
MAIN
SPAR

NAVIGATION LIGHT

AILERON

SINGLE PLYWOOD
SKIN (LOWER)

AILERON
TRIMMING
TAB

LANDING
LIGHT

PETROL
TANK
COVER

FLAP

PITOT
HEAD

RUDDER
MASS
BALANCE

RUDDER
TRIMMING
TAB

ELEVATOR
MASS
BALANCE

RETRACTABLE
TAIL WHEEL

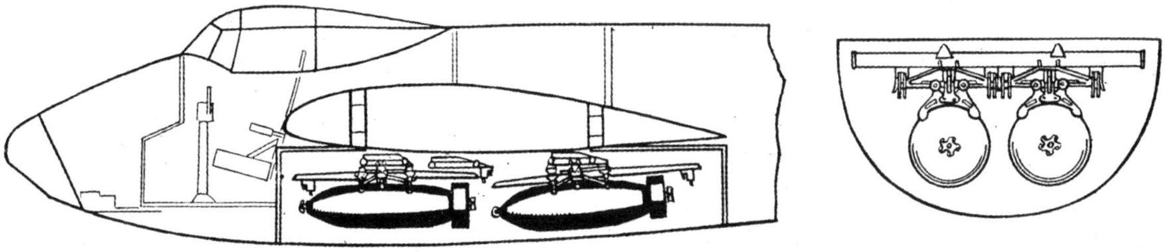

MAX
MILLAR

Side and front elevations of the bomb bay of the bomber version of the Mosquito. The bomb load is 2,000lb. with sufficient fuel to reach most parts of Germany. Four 500lb. bombs are shown. Apart from the arrangement of armament, the fighter and bomber versions are very similar.

'Mossie' in blue

With its superior performance and the ability to avoid interception, the Mosquito was an obvious choice for photographic reconnaissance operations. Martyn Chorlton presents a brief insight of the recce Mosquito - which served the RAF from 1941 to 1955.

RG245, a PR.34 from 540 Squadron, banks away from the camera ship, showing off the PR variant's camera ports. The aircraft also briefly served with 58 Squadron until coming to grief with 540 Squadron at Benson after it swung on take-off on April 5, 1950. *Aeroplane*

A natural choice

When the Mosquito was introduced in 1940, no other operational aircraft came close to the performance figures being achieved by the new de Havilland. Photographic reconnaissance (PR) was a high-priority tasking for the Mosquito and even before the type left the drawing board, one of the three prototypes, W4051, was allocated to the role.

The Mosquito would go on to become the RAF's main, long-range PR aircraft, serving extensively over Europe, Burma, and the South Pacific. With the end of the war there was no let-up in the type's tasking in the photographic role and it was not until the arrival of the Canberra PR.3, that the later marks began to be replaced, although several remained in RAF service in the Far East until late 1955.

Into service, into action

The PR.I prototype, W4051, first flew on June 10, 1941 and, after trials and evaluation at the A&AEE, Boscombe Down, the aircraft was transferred to the PRU (Photographic Development Unit), later 1 PRU, at Benson in Oxfordshire. Only ten PR.Is were built, including the prototype. All initially joined 1 PRU and of those that survived that tour of duty, later served with 69, 521 or 540 Squadron.

The first successful operation was flown on September 20, 1941 by W4055 of 1 PRU, in daylight, photographing enemy facilities at Brest, La Pallice, and Bordeaux before running for home via Paris. The Mosquito did attract the attention of the enemy who despatched three Bf109s to deal with the intruder, but none of the enemy fighters came close on that occasion. However, even the Mosquito's performance did not confer complete invulnerability and, on December 4, 1941, W4055 failed to return from an operation to Trondheim.

By the spring of 1942, 1 PRU was carrying out up to ten sorties per day and the Mosquito's outstanding range meant that targets as far afield as Narvik in the north of Nazi held Europe and the Skoda works at Pilsen in the south could both be reached. To extend the range even further, several airfields were used as forward operating bases. Leuchars and Wick were particular favourites for operations over Norway; St Eval in Cornwall gave the Mosquito more time over France, while Gibraltar allowed the area of operations to expand to cover Northern Africa and Italy as well as providing a useful refuelling point for a return sortie.

Bomber Command was one of 1 PRU's biggest customers, with requests for target photography to aid in planning a raid and for post-raid damage assessment. Finding the locations of enemy warships, especially when they were poised in Atlantic ports, was another favourite Mosquito PR activity and so was locating enemy radar stations; prior to D-Day, more than 70 had been photographed and pinpointed.

By late 1942, 1 PRU could no longer cope with the workload alone, so it was rapidly expanded and divided into four squadrons. Two of these, 540 and 544 Squadron, were both equipped with Mosquitos and, from late 1943, 140 Squadron was re-equipped too.

Expanding the fleet

The Mosquito PR.I had already set the standard and, to help bolster the numbers, a further 27 B.IVs were converted to PR standard. Other than the obvious conversion to accommodate high-altitude cameras, in order to help attain the necessary height, the ex-bomber variant was stripped down to reduce its weight down from 20,900lb to 19,050lb. Improved performance was achieved with the PR.VIII, the first of which was produced by converting B.IV, DZ385 to take a pair of Merlin 61 two-stage supercharged engines. Only five Mosquitoes were converted to PR.VIII standards, Including DZ385, the rest being DZ342, DZ364, DZ404 and DZ424.

With the arrival of the high-altitude B.IX in RAF service, it was a logical step to produce a PR version, the PR.IX, which provided the backbone of the Mosquito recce fleet from May 1943. The latest mark entered service with 540 Squadron and was powered by a pair of Merlin 72/73s or 76/77s. The RAF took delivery of 152 of them.

No place to hide

During mid-1943, more than 3,000 Mosquito PR sorties had been despatched from Benson, free-ranging across Europe with regular visits to Belgrade, Berlin, Budapest, Gdynia, and Vienna. One 540 Squadron sortie, flown on October 3, 1943, brought back the first evidence of the V-1 flying bomb – spotted thanks to the efficiency of photographic interpretation officer, Fg Off Babington Smith, WAAF. The Mosquito had flown over Peenemunde and, to back up what Babington Smith had seen, a further 540 Squadron sortie was flown on November 28. Not long afterwards, RAF Bomber Command paid the weapons testing facility a visit which not only helped to delay development of the V-1 but also the later, more destructive, V-2.

In the Far East, the Mosquito PR was also proving to be a valuable asset and, by the start of 1944, 684 Squadron's aircraft had contributed to an aerial survey of the whole of Burma. By the war's end, Bangkok, Siam, southern Malaya, Singapore, and Japanese held targets in the Dutch East Indies had been photographed.

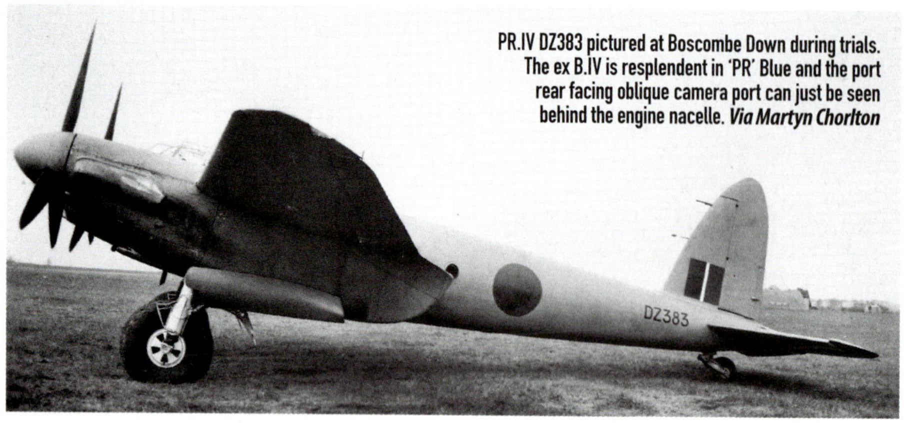

PR.IV DZ383 pictured at Boscombe Down during trials. The ex B.IV is resplendent in 'PR' Blue and the port rear facing oblique camera port can just be seen behind the engine nacelle. *Via Martyn Chorlton*

The solid nose of this RAAF PR Mosquito gives it away as a PR.41 belonging to 87 Squadron. This Australian Official photograph states on the rear, 'A Mosquito aircraft of 87 Survey Squadron of the RAAF taking off from an inland base during survey operations in the Northern Territory. The squadron will eventually make a complete photographic map of 3,000,000 square miles of Australian Territory'. *Australian Official by J Fitzpatrick via Aeroplane*

These continued into the immediate post-war period and one of the longest was flown on August 20, 1945 when a Mosquito flew from the Cocos Islands, photographing Penang and Taiping en route, a flight of approximately 2,600 miles performed in just over nine hours.

The later marks

By late 1943, the Mosquito continued to be developed, resulting in the pressurised, high-altitude bomber variant, the B.XVI. Inevitably, there was a PR version, the prototype, MM258 first flying in July 1943. The PR.XVI was by far the most prolific PR variant, with 432 being built. The mark served with 140 Squadron, 34 (PR) Wing, 2nd TAF (Tactical Air Force) on the continent and all Benson-based PR units.

One spin off variant of the PR.XVI was the PR.32, of which just four were built: NS586-NS589. This rare machine was powered by a pair of Merlin 113 engines and boasted a longer span wing.

The final wartime-built Mosquito PR was another development of the PR.XVI, the PR.34, which was effectively a very long-range version. Designed for use in SEAC (South East Asia Command), where it was thought that an aircraft with a range of over 2,500 miles would be needed. To achieve this, the PR.34 was fitted with a pair of 200 gallon drop tanks under the outer wings and further tankage was installed in the bomb bay. What de Havilland actually achieved, was to design a Mosquito capable of flying 3,500 miles, considerably expanding the

capability of the PR units already operating in the Far East.

Powered by a pair of Merlin 76 or 113 engines, the PR.34 was equipped with a pair of split F.52 vertical cameras, a single oblique F.24 and provision for another pair in the aft position. The first of 181 PR.34s built, made its first flight on December 4, 1944.

Post-war, the PR.34 became the most common type in service with the PR squadrons until the type's withdrawal. Many were upgraded to PR.34A standard by Marshalls of Cambridge Ltd, which involved fitting a pair of Merlin 114A engines, new Gee equipment and a better retraction system for the undercarriage.

The final Mosquito PR was a conversion of the B.35 bomber. The PR.35 was specifically

Mosquito PR.XVI NS519 was delivered direct to the USAAF to serve with the 653rd BS, 25th BG, 325th Photographic Wing at RAF Watton, Norfolk. *Andy Hay/www.flyingart.co.uk*

◀ NS504 from 540 Squadron pictured in June 1944, hence the invasion stripes. Only weeks after this photograph was taken the PR.XVI failed to return from an operation to Lyon on August 6, 1944. *Via Martyn Chorlton*

Mosquito PR.IX MM243 and MM249 of 140 Squadron at Hartford Bridge in early 1944. *Aeroplane*

PR.34 RG300 is pictured in September 1946 during its service with 58 Squadron (later re-numbered 540 Sqn) at Benson. Following conversion to a PR.34A, the Mosquito transferred to 237 and then 231 OCU before being sold for £1,500 in October 1956 and re-registered as N9871F. *Aeroplane*

designed for night time PR operations using powerful photoflashes. Only six were converted, all by de Havilland at their Leavesden plant.

Record breakers

During post-war service, the PR.34 managed to set two incredible air-speed records which comfortably stood until the arrival of the Canberra. The first was achieved on September 6, 1945, when RG241 of 540 Squadron flew from St Mawgan, Cornwall to Gander, Newfoundland in just seven hours. On the return flight, obviously taking advantage of a good tailwind, RG241 flew back to St Mawgan in just five hours and ten minutes.

The second record-breaking PR.34 flight was carried out in May 1947 by Sqn Ldr H B Martin DSO, DFC and his navigator, Sqn Ldr E Sismore DSO, DFC. The flight in Mosquito PR.34, RG238 was from London to Cape Town, South Africa, a distance of 6,717 miles which was carried out in 21 hours 31 minutes and at an average speed of 279mph.

Right to the end of its career, the Mosquito PR.34s carried out excellent work, one highlight being their support of UK rescue services, both military and civilian, during the terrible east coast floods in 1953. Operating from Wyton, the Mosquitos were tasked to photograph damaged coastal walls around Norfolk, Suffolk, and Essex and, in just six days, exposed 16,000 negatives and in short order more than 100,000 prints were processed.

No 81 Squadron was the last RAF unit to operate the PR.34 in Malaya and its final operation was flown on December 15, 1955 by PR.34A RG314; the target, right to the end, was an operational one. ❖

PR VARIANTS

PROTOTYPE AND PR.1 - The first aircraft built could be identified by their short engine nacelles. Power was provided by a pair of Merlin 21 engines.
A/c: W4050 (Prototype), W4051, W4054-4056, W4058-4063 (PR.1)

PR.IV - A B.IV modified for carrying cameras rather than bombs. 32 aircraft are possible candidates for PR.IV conversion but only 27 are officially credited as being converted.
A/c: W4067, DK284, DK310, DK311, DK314, DK315, DK319, DK320, DZ352, DZ357, DZ358, DZ368, DZ382, DZ383, DZ419, DZ431, DZ438, DZ459, DZ466, DZ473, DZ480, DZ487, DZ494, DZ517, DZ523, DZ532, DZ538, DZ544, DZ549, DZ553, DZ592 & DZ596.

PR.VIII - The first Mosquitos capable of operating at high altitude, the PR.VIIIs, were converted from the B.IV but fitted with Merlin 61 engines with two-speed, two-stage superchargers fitted. The aircraft could also be fitted with a pair of 50 gallon wing tanks. Five aircraft converted.
A/c DZ342, DZ364, DZ385 (Prototype), DZ404 and DZ424

PR.IX - Reconnaissance version of the B.IX which served the RAF and 8th Air Force in the meteorological role. A/c LR405-LR481, ML896-ML924 and MM237-MM241

PR.XVI - Photographic-reconnaissance version of the B.XVI fitted with three extra fuel tanks in the bomb bay, cameras in the fuselage and provision of an F.52 to be carrier in converted drop tanks. 432 PR.XVIs were built. A/c ML925-ML999, MM112-MM397, NS496-NS816, RF969-RF999, RG113-RG175 and TA614-TA616.

PR.32 - Lightened version of the PR.XVI fitted with Merlin 113 and 114 two-stage superchargers and extended wing tips for operations at high-altitude.
A/c NS586-NS589.

PR.34 - Long range development of the PR.XVI fitted with Merlin 113 and 114 engines. Capable of 422mph in level flight; making it the fastest of all production Mosquitos. 181 built. A/c PF620-PF680, RG176-RG318 and VL613-VL625

PR.34A - Modernised version of the PR.34 with a revised cockpit layout.

PR.35 - Six aircraft converted from B.35s to PR.35 standard.
A/c RS700, TK650, VP183 & VR803-VR805.

PR.40 - Australian-built photographic reconnaissance conversion of the FB.40 with Packard-Merlin engines. These half-dozen machines served as a stopgap, pending the arrival of the PR.XVI.
A/c A52-2, A52-4, A52-6, A52-7, A52-9 & A52-56.

PR.41 - Australian-built photographic reconnaissance version of the FB.40 with additional radio equipment and a pair of Packard-Merlin 69 two-stage, supercharged engines. The PR.41 had a solid nose and carried five cameras, one of them in the nose, two verticals and a pair of obliques in the rear fuselage. 28 PR Mk 41s were built, all of them serving during the post-war years.
A/c A52-36, A52-41, A52-45, A52-49, A52-62, A52-64, A52-83, A52-90, A52-192-A52-211.

TECHNICAL SPECIFICATIONS PR.34

POWERPLANT: Two 1,710hp Rolls-Royce Merlin 76 or 113

DIMENSIONS: Span, 54ft 2in; length, 41ft 6in; height, 15ft 3in; wing area, 454sq ft

WEIGHTS: Empty, 16,631lb; loaded 25,500lb

PERFORMANCE: Max speed, 425mph at 30,500ft; cruising speed, 325mph at 30,000ft; range 3,500 miles; service ceiling, 36,000ft

ARMAMENT: Nil

Ground crew remove all ve F.52 cameras (for the benet of the photographer) from PR.34 RG245 at Benson in 1948. On April 5, 1950, RG245 swung on take-off causing the undercarriage to collapse; the aircraft was not repaired. *Aeroplane*

Rangers and Insteps

Alastair Goodrum describes 25 Squadron Mosquito operations over Northern Germany and Biscay in the spring and summer of 1943.

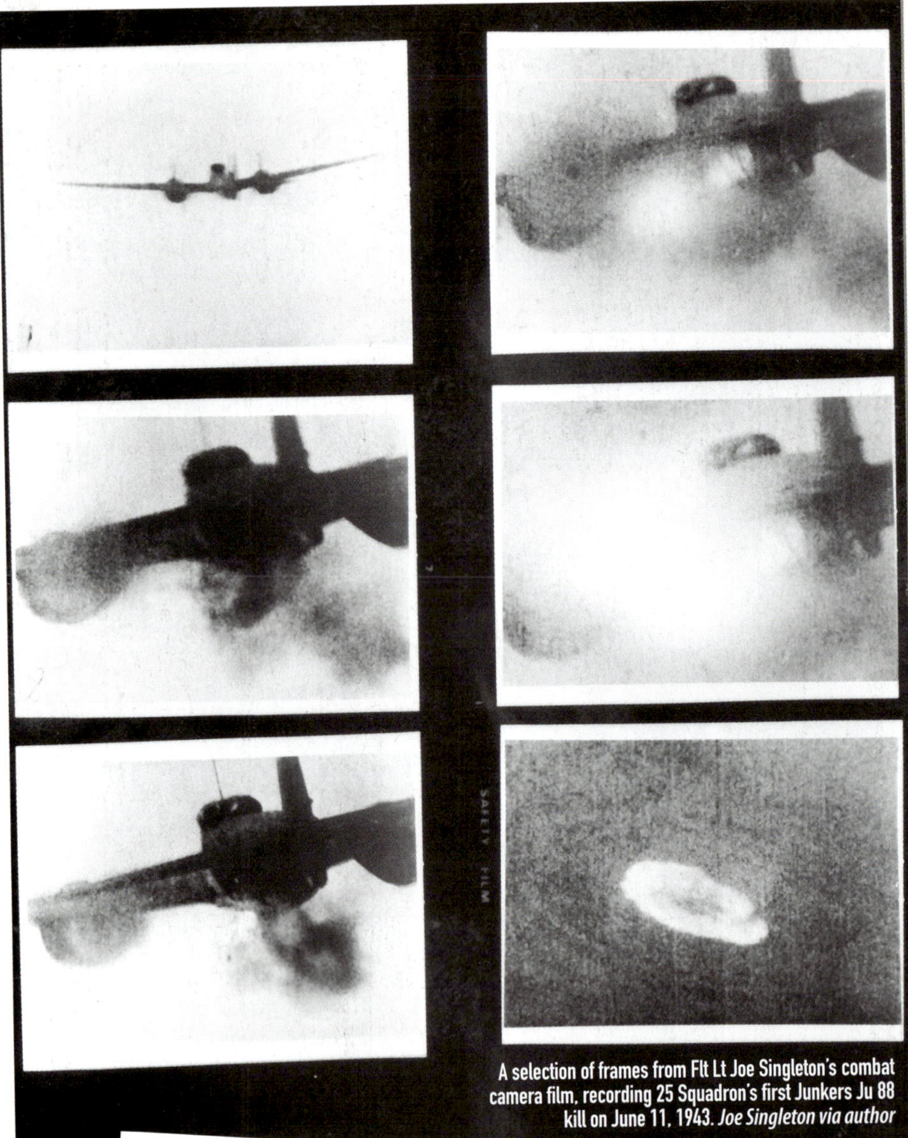

A selection of frames from Flt Lt Joe Singleton's combat camera film, recording 25 Squadron's first Junkers Ju 88 kill on June 11, 1943. *Joe Singleton via author*

▲ Fg Off Jack Cheney, pilot with 25 Squadron, Church Fenton circa 1943. *Via author*

Fg Off Bill Carnaby pictured whilst serving with 85 Squadron. He was a flight commander in 25 Squadron in 1943. *Via author* ➤

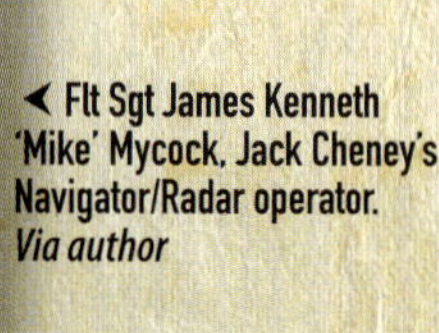

◄ Flt Sgt James Kenneth 'Mike' Mycock, Jack Cheney's Navigator/Radar operator. *Via author*

Mosquito NF.II, W4076 in RDM2 black night-fighter camouflage, at Boscombe Down on February 25, 1942. The fighter went on to serve with 60 OTU, 141, 169 and 239 Squadrons, 1692 Flight and 54 OTU before being SOC on June 5, 1945. *Via Martyn Chorlton*

A new posting

Just four weeks after his 21st birthday, Fg Off Jack Cheney was posted to Church Fenton, home to the Mosquito NF.IIs of 25 Squadron. Arriving on January 29, 1943 he was to convert to the twin-engine night-fighter and posted in with him was his navigator/radio observer ('RO'), radar operator W/O James 'Mike' Mycock. Jack recalls some of their Mosquito sorties over northern Europe and the Bay of Biscay during 1943.

Freelance Rangers

Next morning all the new arrivals at Church Fenton were introduced to the Squadron Commander, Wg Cdr E G Watkins AFC, who spelled out why we were here and what was expected of us. He explained that, back in 1942, moves were made to use Mossies on intruder operations, as a more effective replacement for Douglas Boston's then in service. Supply of Mosquitoes for this purpose was, however, slow and only a handful were made available for intruding by the close of that year.First priority was given to the night fighter defence force but, in the light of a decline in the enemy's night-time forays, in December 1942 the role of the force was revised and more of them were allocated for offensive 'ops'.

Wg Cdr Watkins outlined how the crews of 25 Squadron were to intensify their training with the objective of undertaking freelance sorties known as Rangers. 12 Group, into which Church Fenton fell, was allocated northern Germany as its 'patch' and the intruder sorties would be operated from forward aerodromes which were to be Coltishall and Castle Camps.

Night Rangers were sorties against transport targets, mounted during the moon periods when it was possible to see the ground more clearly. Intruder sorties, on the other hand, were those made in the dark periods, involving patrols in the vicinity of one or more enemy airfields and setting off at predetermined times. At set times other aircraft would take over from those despatched earlier, so that a constant patrol could be maintained in order to restrict enemy aircraft movements. The whole idea was to keep the Hun on his toes all the time, to disrupt his communications and destroy aircraft and other transport in the process. One Flight would fly Rangers on moonlight nights while the other Flight would still be required to put up the usual defensive patrols and vice versa.

It all sounded terrific stuff and Mike and I were allocated to 'A' Flight. During the afternoon we new boys were given 'gen' on the Mosquito by our flight commander Sqn Ldr Bill Carnaby. I finished off that busy day by swotting up the Pilot's Notes during the evening and again the next morning. Early in February there began the first of many lectures on navigation to a level essential for 'swanning about' over northern Europe. A bit of a setback occurred when, with an already poor serviceability record, the dual Mosquito T.III, HJ862, pranged into a dispersal bay and went u/s yet again. My 'A' Flight colleague Joe Singleton, however, was authorised to give me a trip in his Mossie, during which we actually contrived to swap seats in the air! It was not long afterwards that I was officially checked out in the dual Mossie and Mike and I went onto the operational crew roster at last.

Long Ranger Loco busting

April 1943 saw the start of the offensive *Night Ranger* operations by 25 Squadron using some of our Mosquito NF.IIs with the AI radar removed; a Gee navigation set installed; an extra fuel tank and more cannon ammo. Mike and I got our first taste of the action on April 20, 1943 with a brace of trains, then we were in the thick of the action again on May 15 when we took off from our forward base at Coltishall on *Long Ranger* Route No.1.

Take off was at 2310hrs. A large convoy of ships was seen off Vlieland and I overflew them in a diving turn without stirring up a nasty greeting, before crossing the Dutch coast a few minutes later.We reached a familiar pin point at Makkum then headed for the Diepholtz area where I orbited the airfield looking for trade. After stooging around for ten minutes without any sign of life, Mike spotted a train entering the town from the south. I peeled off into a shallow dive and raked it from abeam with a three-second burst of cannon fire, breaking off at 500ft with strikes being seen all over the coaches.It was essential for Mike to keep calling out the altitude during these diving attacks as it was quite impossible to concentrate on the gunsight and the target and watch our height all at the same time, for one could become quite mesmerised by the kaleidoscope of dials, flashes and explosions.

Turning away now towards Steinhuder Lake, lights were seen at Lengenhagen aerodrome on the outskirts of Hanover but we were out of luck, for no aeroplane activity was detected there. Two searchlights probed the sky from Burgdorf aerodrome in an effort to catch us but they did not illuminate our aircraft. Shortly after this, two trains were sighted near Gifhorn and I hammered both these one after the other in beam attacks using raking three-second bursts from the cannon only. Several strikes were observed on both locomotives and after the second pass, the sky was lit up by a satisfying red glow as we left them behind.

We pressed on towards Gardelegen airfield, only 70 miles short of Berlin and en route, surprised another train west of Fallersleben. I made two runs at this one, firing a short burst on the first pass from astern then whipping hard round and pouring a longer burst from all eight guns along the whole length of the train, watching the cannon shells hitting the coaches and loco on each pass. During the second attack there was moderate but accurate light *flak* coming at us from the nearby town, so we sheared off and set course for Salzwedel airfield. A few minutes later, another train was spotted near Wieren and I made two head-on attacks with the cannon, producing strikes on the locomotive both times.

Now we turned north in the general direction of Hamburg. A couple of minutes after passing over Ulzen a train hove into view outside Unterlutz. Running in from behind this time, I gave it a three-second burst from the machine guns only and hung on so long in the dive that the *Mossie* was almost skimming the rear end of the train by the time I hauled the nose up. Saw good hits on the leading coaches and the loco.

After this last attack the windscreen misted over on the outside, which made navigation difficult so, since our ammo was just about finished, Mike gave me a course for base via the Zuider Zee at Aarderwijk and the Dutch coast at Ijmuiden. The return was uneventful and we touched down at Coltishall at 0320hrs to claim in our four-hour sortie five locomotives and an unknown quantity of coaches on which I had expended 700 rounds of 20mm and 1,000 rounds of .303in ammo. Two other *Ranger* crews (Haigh/Ellacott and Singleton/Skinner) also claimed a further four trains between them but 25 Squadron's two *Intruder* sorties to the Soesterberg (F/O Wooton) and Deelen (P/O Cooke) airfield areas each drew a blank. On the whole it had been a productive night though and I slept the sleep of the exhausted.

Ranger Route No.19

Four nights later Mike and I were off again, this time allocated to *Ranger* Route No.19. We were second away, after Fg Off Davies who went to the Drentewede area. Keeping low over the North Sea, then climbing to 4,500ft to cross the coast at Terschelling at midnight, Mike gave me a course for Assen, Aschendorf, Syke and Drackenburg and skirting round the hot spot of Bremen. Searching in a north-east direction we sighted a train a few miles east of Visselhovede and I immediately dived at it

head-on, letting go with a three-second burst of cannon. This hit the locomotive which promptly rolled to a stop emitting lovely dense clouds of smoke and steam. One down! We turned away for Soltau then headed east to Ulzen, attacking a southbound train near Bevensen. This loco was hammered with cannon fire and it, too, was left stationary, in clouds of steam lit up by a dull red glow.

We took time now to patrol up and down the Ulzen to Hannover railway line looking for 'trade'. Our luck was in since, before long, we

were rewarded by the sight of no less than *three* trains near Celle. No time to dither. I hit the first loco with cannon fire in a head-on attack and the second, a few miles behind it and travelling in the same direction, was given the same treatment. Quickly hauling the Mossie round in a tight turn I overtook the third train. I came at this one from behind and raked its whole length with a four-second burst from the combined fire power of the cannon and Brownings. This loco was hit and ground to a halt, erupting in large clouds of

Mosquito NF.II, DD737 showing off the nose-mounted arrowhead transmitter antenna for AI Mk V radar, and the wingtip 'rod' receiver antennas. The censor routinely deleted these sensitive antennae from released photos. This aircraft was operated by 85 Squadron during 1942, then by 264 Squadron in 1943 before being passed to 54OTU. She went missing on a training flight on December 6, 1944. *Via author*

A well-known but censored photo of Mosquito NF.II, DD750 of 25 Squadron with the AI Mk V antennae carefully deleted. This aircraft was lost on March 22, 1943 when it flew into a hill near Keighley, West Yorkshire. *Via author*

Flt Lt Joe Singleton (Left) and his Radio Operator, Fg Off Geoff Haslam of 25 Squadron. *Via author* ▾

steam and smoke.

This area was proving to be very fruitful as yet another train was observed five miles away puffing serenely towards Celle. I dived on this one from head-on, firing at it with machine guns only and hits seemed to pepper the loco and set fire to some of the coaches, which were burning furiously as the train came to a halt.

Squadron and RAF record

Having stirred up a hornet's nest Mike, always on top of our position, gave me a course to steer for base. As we flew over Steinhuder Lake, sadly low on fuel and ammunition, some ten miles or so to the north could be seen what appeared to be an aerodrome with signs of a visual Lorenz lighting system. However, keeping on track we came across another train on the outskirts of Lemforde and with some ammunition left it was too good a target to overlook. I dived straight at it and let fly a concentrated burst with the remaining Browning ammo, which produced the usual clouds of steam and a satisfying red glow. Time to go home.

The rest of the flight back had to be by dead reckoning as the compass had packed up after the last attack. We must have wandered off course a bit near Utrecht because the aircraft was suddenly coned by about twelve searchlights. They held us for a couple of minutes before I could throw them off with violent evasive action. The lights were followed up by a barrage of intense and pretty accurate light flak but we emerged unscathed. Ten minutes later, as we crossed the Dutch coast, we were picked up by two more searchlights on the island of Overflakee. They held us for about a minute and it was only by more violent manoeuvres and then diving full pelt to the deck that they were shaken off. I kept down low over the North Sea and we

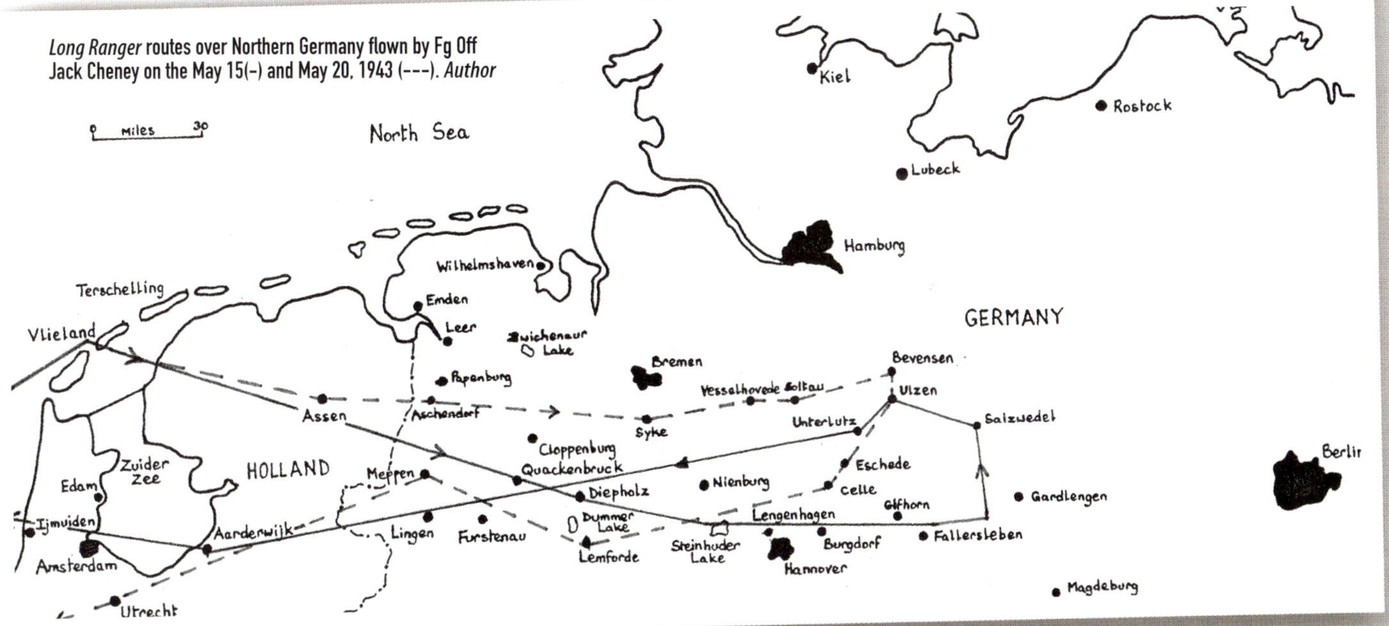

landed at Coltishall at 0335hrs after another four hours of working up quite a sweat. This time our claim was for seven locomotives and an unknown number of coaches set on fire. [Author: seven locos by one crew in one night sortie was a 25 Squadron record and also remained unbeaten by any other squadron in WW2.]

Wg Cdr Simon Maude - squadron CO since March - was one of the other *Ranger* crews that night. He had been busy in the Bremen area, claiming one train and starting fires in a factory and rail yard during his sortie. In contrast, Sqn Ldr Francis Brinsden saw no activity whatsoever and his description of his own sortie was highly original, in that he became the first pilot to complain of boredom on a *Ranger* operation!

Things remained quiet until June 4 when orders were received for three crews, complete with their aircraft, to be dispatched for special duties at Predannack. This mysterious project captured everyone's imagination and the crews selected were mine; Flt Lt Joe Singleton with Fg Off Geoff Haslam and Fg Off Wootton with Plt Off Dymock. That same day was spent in preparing ourselves and our aircraft to leave but rain and low cloud prevented departure.

Insteps for Coastal Command

Much of the following day was spent swinging the compasses and re-harmonising the guns of Mosquitoes assigned to the Predannack operation: DZ688, DZ685 and my aircraft DD757, which were from among those employed on *Ranger* operations. By teatime on June 5 the wind freshened but the clouds

lifted sufficiently to allow us to embark on our detachment to 264 Squadron's base.

It was made clear that the main task of these composite squadron operations, code named *Instep*, is to patrol the Bay of Biscay in an attempt to intercept and destroy enemy aircraft, notably Ju88s, that were interfering with Coastal Command's anti-submarine patrols. No time was lost and we were to begin ops immediately. At 1800hrs in the evening of June 7 Joe Singleton with his navigator Geoff Haslam and I with Mike, took off in company with two other Mossies from 456 Squadron and headed south across the wide open spaces of the Bay of Biscay.

It was strange flying over the expanse of the sea, out of sight of land for so long, heading ever further south towards the north coast of Spain. After an uneventful flight in loose formation we turned at the end of the patrol line at latitude 46.00N, longitude 04.15W. Coming round onto the northerly heading I spotted a smudge of smoke to starboard and reported it to Joe who was formation leader. Altering course, our formation came up with a fishing vessel that was identified as a French trawler named *Tadorne*. We had been briefed to watch out for such vessels, as they were suspected of passing on information about Coastal Command aircraft to the Ju88 units. Since all fishing vessels had been warned by leaflet drops to keep out of the area Joe had no hesitation in going in to attack.

Ordering me and one of the 456 boys to orbit as top cover, Joe told Plt Off John Newell of 456 to go line astern and follow him down

to attack. They each carried out two strafing runs on the vessel and hits were registered all over the centre of the target, which stopped dead in the water, on fire and with clouds of smoke and steam billowing from it. We reformed on Joe's aircraft and returned to Predannack without further incident. [research revealed that the Vichy vessel *Tadorne* operated from La Rochelle and was pressed into German Navy service as UJ-2218 in the role of an armed auxiliary sub-hunter. The attack took place 110 nautical miles west of La Pallice, during which the trawler was badly damaged with casualties of three dead and five injured but despite this damage, the vessel managed to return to La Rochelle.]

Hunting Ju88s over the bay

There was yet more excitement a couple of days later when I was part of a patrol that made contact with five Ju88s over the Bay. In the ensuing fracas, one Ju88 was destroyed by Joe Singleton: the first 'kill' by a 25 Squadron Mosquito.

Our patrol of six Mosquitoes, led by Joe, took off from Predannack during the afternoon of June 11. Jimmy Wootton was flying as No.2, I was No.3 and three of the 456 crews made up the second section. Shortly after takeoff, Flt Lt Gordon Panitz of 456 had to break away and return to base with engine trouble while the rest of us continued on our way in a loose vic formation at sea level. When nearing the end of the outward leg, about 130 miles off the north-west tip of Spain, Jimmy spotted a formation of five Ju88s through the broken cloud, flying in loose echelon at 5,000ft almost directly above us. Well, this was what we had come for.

Immediately Joe ordered our formation to close up and started a climb up-sun of the enemy. He called for Jimmy Wootton (25) and John Newell (456) to stay with him and for me (25) to take Flt Sgt Richardson (456) and operate as a separate section and keep an eye out for the Ju88's own top cover. However, at this point my radio decided to pack up so, although Richardson closed up on me we were unable to make contact with the enemy before the Ju88s broke off the engagement. Later, Joe told me what happened.

He said his section was seen by the enemy early in the climb to get up-sun. The enemy started a climbing orbit in loose line astern, firing off red star-flares as they did so. Joe replied by firing of his own Very pistol in the hope of adding to the confusion and gain time to claw more height. Both formations tried to turn up-sun of each other and when the enemy aircraft were about 2,000ft above, he gave the order to break formation and for everyone to pick their own target. Several of the enemy opened fire but Joe, selecting the rearmost, turned inside it and opened fire with a full deflection shot from 800yds. The burst hit the Ju88's port engine and thick smoke poured out. Further bursts of cannon brought even more flames and smoke and the enemy aircraft turned slowly over onto its back and dived into the sea, where a large oil patch marked its entry. Jimmy Wootton and John Newell between them claimed three more Ju88s as damaged before they hightailed it off home. ✤

Mosquito NF.II, DD739 of 456 Sqn as used on *Instep* patrols in 1943 with AI Mk V radar removed from nose but wing antennae retained.
Via Martyn Chorlton

Map showing Bay Of Biscay *Instep* patrol area and contacts made during Jack Cheney's sorties in June 1943. *Author* ➤

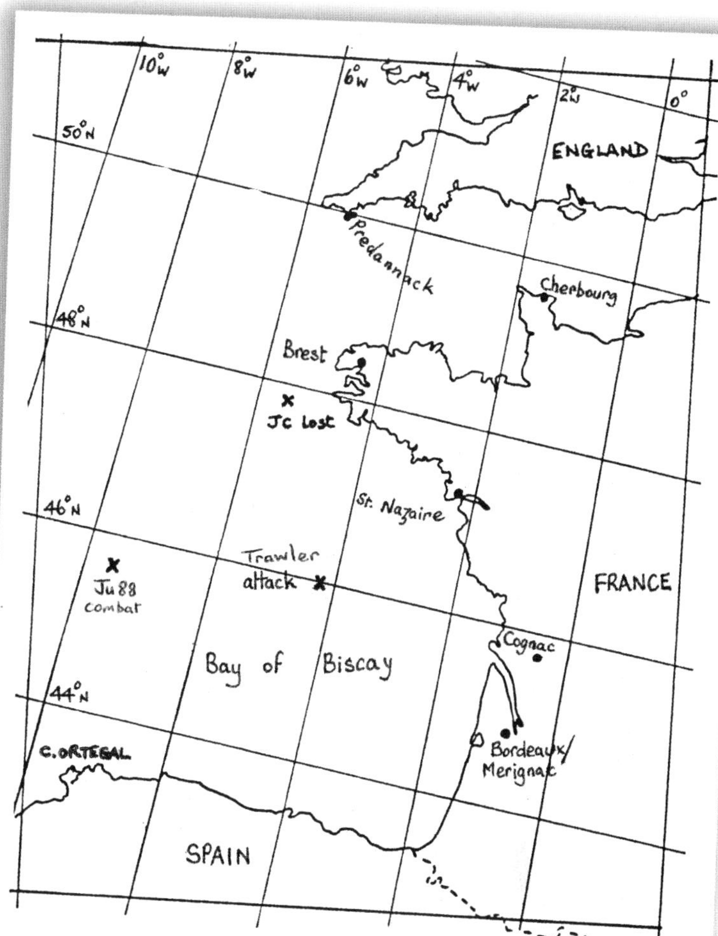

25 Squadron at Church Fenton on June 16, 1943. From left: Seated front: Lloyd Davies; Sqn Ldr Freddie Snell; Wg Cdr Simon Maude (CO); Gp Capt Frank Stannard (Stn Cdr); Joe Singleton; Ron Cooke. Middle: Benny Bent; Tommy Gibbs; Bill Cummings; George Hogarth; Freddie Haigh; Jack Cairns; Norris; Grey; Harry Gallacgher, Gus Guthrie; n/k; n/k. Back: Franklin; Cooke; Norman Underdown; Pete Sewell; n/k; n/k; Dennis Skinner; n/k; Frank Charman. ▼

A Mosquito NF.II of 25 Squadron photographed at RAF Church Fenton in early 1943. 25 Squadron first received the Mosquito NF.II in October 1942 until January 1944, the FB.VI, NF.30 and NF.36 followed until replaced by the Vampire NF.10 in July 1951. *Aeroplane*

COLOUR key
Breaking Down Points
Plywood Surfaces
Solid and Laminated Spruce Construction
Spruce Struts, Balsa Filling Birch Ply Skin
Ash Stiffeners (Main Spar)
Metal Structure
Balsa Wood Planking 
RTP
MOSQUITO ma
FOR FURTHER INFORMATION SEE A.P. 2019 & 2653 (VOL. II PART 3). NOTE T

1. Fuselage
2. Main Plane
3. Flaps
4. Ailerons
5. Wing Tips
6. Aileron Trimmer Tabs
7. Power Units
8. Undercarriage
9. Fin
10. Rudder
11. Rudder Trimmer Tabs
12. Tail Plane
13. Elevator
14. Elevator Trimmer Tabs
15. Retractable Tail Wheel
AIR DIAGRAM 3209
SHEET No. 1
No. OF SHEETS 1
JAN. 1945
AL No.
AMENDMENTS MADE
INITIALS DATE
PREPARED BY
MINISTRY OF AIRCRAFT PRODUCTION
FOR PROMULGATION BY
AIR MINISTRY

n structure

ER IS ILLUSTRATED BUT STRUCTURE, IN THE MAIN, IS IDENTICAL ON ALL MARKS

Armourers reloading 20mm shells for the Mosquito NF.II's quartet of Hispano cannon. *Aeroplane* ➤

The Mosquito night fighter packed four 20mm cannon under the fuselage and four .303in machine guns under the nose. *Via Aeroplane*

The Fighting Mosquito Squadron

264 Squadron's seamless transition from the Defiant to the Mosquito was described by 'S.V.' on May 21, 1943, in *The Aeroplane*.

Defiant makes way

WITH MOSQUITO fighters coming off the assembly lines in swarms, the Air Ministry has lately had the pleasant task of selecting squadrons to fly them. One squadron upon which the choice fell formerly flew Defiants. It is, in fact, the squadron which shocked the Luftwaffe over Dunkirk in May, 1940, by shooting down a whole Staffel of Messerschmitt Me 110s before breakfast and ending the day with the record bag of 37 confirmed victories (post-war German records reduced this to a still creditable 14 victories).

The squadron received its Mosquitoes nearly a year ago and has now attacked and damaged 43 locomotives, shot down two Junkers Ju 88s and damaged one and probably damaged another; probably destroyed a Heinkel He 111, damaged a Do

217, shot up 10 power stations and electrical transformers, wrecked a number of lorries, made some 60 individual patrols over the Bay of Biscay and some 70 day and night intrusions, mostly into France.

Pilots had no trouble in acquiring the Mosquito technique. Those who were not accustomed to twins were given brief spells on Oxfords; those who were, studied the Mosquito manual and forthwith took off. This was not the hazardous adventure that might be imagined. There are no tricks to learn, no vices to master, no disconcerting habits to be watched. In the Mosquito, the pilots discovered the responsiveness of the Tiger Moth, and in it powerful motors, swift acceleration and great speed, not added dangers, but new and exhilarating sources of pleasure.

Under the Mossie's spell

They soon found themselves beneath the Mosquito's spell. To them, it is well-nigh flawless. They admit of no equivalent and would refuse any substitute. They eagerly accept every mission that comes to them because they know that they have every chance of fulfilling it and returning. They rate it an honour that they were among the first to receive the Mosquito and they are prepared, on occasion, to show their skill to their friends, without 'effects,' as readily as they are to the enemy with them. They welcomed the opportunity to 'show us the works' when we visited them recently.

In diving on the control tower and shooting it up with silent guns they showed faultless judgment. At their speed, an error of a hair's breadth or of the smallest conceivable

One of the first Mosquito NF.IIs to join 264 Squadron was W4081 'PS-R' in the background. The fighter survived its tour of duty with 264 Squadron and went on to also serve with 307, 157 and 51 OTU before retiring in February 1946. *Aeroplane*

portion of the time would have been fatal, but with all the ease, grace and carelessness imaginable, they deftly lifted themselves up and over the heads of the roof-top watchers and swung away on steeply banked wings into the cold grey sky of a Spring afternoon. It was not a crazy exhibition, but flying of a kind that makes admiration breathless.

They had used most of the runway for the take-off, preferring they said, the asset of speed to that of height. A little flap would have made them airborne earlier, but they refrained from using it. Nor were the motors fully extended; there still remained a good margin in hand. Full throttle running is uneconomic and shortens a motor's life. Over enemy territory a few minutes later, the Mosquito might want all that the motor can give, and worn parts mean lost power.

The pilots always fly with a navigator. A sortie may send a Mosquito 600 miles from its base - perhaps at tree-top or wave-crest height all the way. Piloting, then, is a full-time occupation. The man at the helm must have his eyes outside the cockpit; a momentary glance at a map or a compass might mean disaster. The navigators are chosen for the speed and accuracy of their calculations.

At first some of the navigators found the Mosquito's speed excessive. One, bound at

night for a well-defended aerodrome is France, announced to his pilot that they would soon be there. The aerodrome they were seeking at once corrected the navigator by filling the sky around with a great fury of 'flak.' It was the defence, not the attackers, who scored the surprise.

Speed is but one of the Mosquito's virtues. Armament is another. In the belly are four cannon; in the nose, four machine-guns. The machine-guns are normally reserved for 'soft skin' targets such as motor lorries, the wooden huts of military camps, and enemy troops. The cannon disable locomotives, prise open armoured cars, smash canal lock gates, wreck dynamos and transformers, and destroy aircraft. The choice of cannon or machine-guns, or both, is made through a selector switch in the cockpit.

In a dog fight the fighter version of the Junkers Ju 88 is poor sport for the Mosquito. Three Mosquitoes caught a pair of them over the Bay of Biscay searching for Coastal Command bombers on anti-submarine patrol. In the brief engagement which followed the two enemy fighters were shot down with little ceremony. All three-Mosquitos had a hand in the slaughter, but a pilot who was there said that one Mosquito could have coped with the situation. That remark was not a boast. Nor was it line-shooting. It was a modest tribute to a great aeroplane expressed as a fact.

Smiling in the face of danger

Any attempt here to describe all the virtues of the Mosquito would be merely to send a faint echo bounding off the mountain of praise already heaped upon it by those who fly and fight with it. To quote the epic 400 miles' flight home on one motor, made by the squadron's commanding officer, to describe the lightness of the damage caused by ground fire to the wood structure, and to record the crews' satisfaction with their cockpit would be merely to extol qualities already extolled.

Of all modern aeroplanes, the Mosquito must be confessed the fittest subject for commendation. In its shapely fuselage it compounds the elements of fury, havoc and destruction. In its speed it stretches the enemy's defences to the utmost. In its range it lengthens Fighter Command's arm, and in its construction it makes the smallest calls upon our precious stocks of metal.

To talk with the pilots and navigators of this squadron is to learn the meaning of high morale. Suggest that their work is fraught with danger and they smile. Hint that they need frequent rests from operations to recover their nerve and they are scandalised. They are eager to be off on sorties and would have taken a dim view of the Press visit which kept them on the ground for the better part of the day had the weather been right for locomotive hunting.

Mosquito NF.II DD636 during its service with 264 Squadron. The fighter was transferred to 307 and finally 157 Squadron and on November 19, 1943 had to be ditched into the Bay of Biscay following an engine failure. *Andy Hay/www.flyingart.co.uk*

Their ground crews, too, are in high humour. They await the return of their Mosquitoes, paint pot in hand it seems, ready to emblazon the nose with the symbols of the latest targets. No academician ever worked with greater zest than the man who paints the little white and brown railway engines - white for daylight victims, brown for night - for all the squadron to see. When the nose of the machine carries the picture of a locomotive yard - and several do - the ground crew is apt to swagger.

If the same spirit pervades other Mosquito fighter squadrons - and it unquestionably does - then, indeed, the enemy has plenty to fear. These young fellows, keen and aggressive and working in paired partnerships, are proud of their squadron and proud of the work it is doing. And in the Mosquito fighter they have a mighty foundation for their pride. ✤

264 SQUADRON IN BRIEF

OCTOBER 30	1939	Formed at Sutton Bridge
DECEMBER	1939	Received Defiant I
SEPTEMBER	1941	Received Defiant II
MAY	1942	Received Mosquito NF.II
AUGUST	1943	Received Mosquito FB.VI
DECEMBER	1943	Received Mosquito NF.XIII
AUGUST 25	1945	Disbanded at B106/Twente
NOVEMBER 20	1945	Reformed at Church Fenton with Mosquito NF.30
MARCH	1946	Received Mosquito NF.36
NOVEMBER	1951	Received Meteor NF.11
OCTOBER	1954	Received Meteor NF.14
SEPTEMBER 30	1957	Disbanded at Leeming

46 bombing operations and four enemy locomotives destroyed credited to this 264 Squadron Mosquito. The symbols in black were carried out at night and the two in white, during the day. *Via Martyn Chorlton*

An NF.30 which was equipped with the American AI Mk X radar; originally known as the SCR 720. To the right of the pilot's instruments is (from the top) the radar operator's Indicator (Operators (BC–1151–B)) unit which has two screens. One shows the relative height of the target while the other displays the relative bearing. The operator can adjust a range marker line up and down on the screen to select the desired target on the right hand screen. Once the marker line is over the target it appears on the left hand screen, also known as the 'C' Tube. The next unit down is a Synchronizer (BC–1148–D) and below that is the Control Box (BC–1342); these were used for the SCR 729 secondary radar for navigation.
Aeroplane

10,000 Cookies!

The Light Night Striking Force by Martyn Chorlton

Mosquito IVs of 139 Squadron at Marham in early 1943. DZ464 (left centre) was shot down by flak over the French coast on May 21, 1943 while returning from Orleans. Sqn Ldr V R G Harcourt DFC and WO J Friendly DFM were both killed. *Via author*

Mosquito IVs of 139 Squadron at Marham prepare to depart on another operation. Nearest to the camera is DZ421, which was lost after take-off on a NAVEX with 1655 MTU (Mosquito Training Unit) on July 25, 1944. Next to it is DZ373, which went missing on an operation to Liège, not long after this photograph was taken on March 12, 1943. *Via author*

The early days of Oboe

The story of the Light Night Striking Force (LNSF) is one that began in late May 1943 when 2 Group ceased to be a part of Bomber Command. Thanks to the foresight of Air Commodore Don Bennett, two of the former 2 Group Mosquito units, 105 and 139 Squadrons were transferred to his new 8 (Pathfinder Force) Group. The seeds were now sown for a new approach to the Bomber Command offensive, making use of the Mosquito's, speed, and range, to give the Pathfinders a more survivable platform to mark targets for the Main Force bombers.

Mosquitos had been a part of 8 Group since August 1942 when 109 Squadron was transferred to it from the WIDU (Wireless Intelligence Development Unit). The squadron had been quietly working in the background developing and testing the bomb aiming system Oboe, initially using the Wellington B.IV, but the equipment did not like the transition to the Mosquito. Problems with the equipment were not fully resolved until June 1943 but

Mosquito IV DZ637 began its service with 627 Squadron in late 1943. After a short spell with 692 Squadron the bomber returned to Oakington and 8 Group only to be lost on an operation to Siegen on February 2, 1945. *Via author* ▾

Bennetts' impatience and the keenness displayed by the crews of 109 Squadron resulted in Oboe entering service before it was completely mature.

At 1755hrs on December 20, 1942, Sqn Ldr H E Bufton and his navigator Flt Lt E L I Fould led six Mosquitos against the Lutterade power station. On approaching the target, it was Bufton who dropped the first Oboe-aimed bombs along with two other crews from the small formation. The Oboe transmitter in the remaining three aircraft failed to work properly and they bombed elsewhere, a familiar story to those who had been working on the project for many months. Post attack reconnaissance flown the following day over Lutterade was unable to establish whether the Oboe attack had been successful because of craters from a previous raid. Local reports stated that nine bombs fell in open country approximately a mile from the power station and very close to a large area of housing. However, the system would prove to be invaluable as the war progressed and, by June 1943, 8 Group introduced 105 Squadron as its second Oboe-equipped unit.

No 139 Squadron's motto, 'We destroy at Will' had become very appropriate since receiving its first Mosquito IV back in June 1942. Twelve months later, the squadron was doing just that and, on June 13/14, 1943, 13 of the unit's Mosquitos set out to bomb Berlin, Dusseldorf, and Cologne for its first operation as part of 8 Group. The raid was a bit of an anti-climax as all three cities were cloud-covered and only estimated positions were bombed. What was significant about the raid was the fact that all aircraft returned safely, without harassment by night fighters or flak, in half the time that a four engined heavy would have taken.

After gaining further experience flying 'nuisance' raids during June and into mid-July, 139 Squadron was tasked with dropping Window – strips of chaff intended to 'blind' enemy radar - ahead of a large raid for the first time. The target on July 25/26 was Essen, with 705 aircraft taking part including 19 Mosquitos at the front, flying alongside the seasoned PFF crews. As the target was approached, the Mosquitos began dropping Window on their first run and then went around again to bomb the target. Four nights later, the squadron's Mosquitos dropped Window over Hamburg ahead of the marker crews.

Spoofing!

Another new tactic thanks to the increased involvement of the Mosquito was the

Mosquitos of 627 Squadron at Oakington in March 1944, only weeks before they were transferred to 5 Group at Woodhall Spa. *Via author*

introduction of the diversion raid or 'spoofing'. The first time this was tried out was on the night of August 10/11 when the main force of 653 bombers attacked Nuremberg. Meanwhile, just nine Mosquitos carried out their 'spoof' on Mannheim, dropping Window on the run in and also dropping TIs (Target Indicators) for the first time. The small force then made two extra runs on the target, dropping HE as they went. While losses were average on the Nuremberg raid, the effect of the diversion could not be fully gauged, but on the night of August 17/18, the spoof certainly made a difference. The target on this occasion was Peenemünde and if the enemy's night fighter controllers got a sniff of this target being attacked, then most of the Luftwaffe's finest would be directed towards them. A force of 596 Lancasters, Halifaxes and Stirlings headed for the German Research Establishment while eight Mosquitos set course for Berlin. Once over the German capital, the first two of three waves were already preparing to attack Peenemünde, completely unmolested by the enemy except for local flak defences. This could be credited to the highly successful diversion by 139 Squadron who had duped the enemy fighter controllers into thinking that Berlin was the main target. To the enemy's credit, they reacted extremely fast when they had realised their error and the third wave of bombers would bear the brunt of the night's losses'; but it could have been so much worse. Even 139 Squadron did not completely get away with it, losing two aircraft by the end of the night. Fg Off A S Cooke and Sgt D A H Dixon in Mosquito B.IV DZ379 were intercepted by a night-fighter and shot down near Berge, killing both crew instantly. The second loss was more fortunate for the crew when Flt Lt R A V Crampton and Fg

Mosquito IV DZ344 after a wheels up landing at Oakington in March 1944. The Mosquito was repaired and later served with 2 Group CS, 21 Squadron and finally 140 Wing before being SOC on June 12, 1945. *Via author*

Off P L U Cross were both injured after DZ465 crash-landed at Swanton Morely.

When it was the turn of the bombers to hit Berlin again on the night of September 30/October 1, several of the crews reported seeing white flares along the route in and out of the target. These were presumed to have been initiated by the Germans to guide their defensive fighters towards the main bomber stream – a tactic the Luftwaffe christened 'Wild Boar'. A dangerous game of cat and mouse had been initiated and on the next trip to Berlin on September 3/4, Mosquitos dropped their own white flares at intervals, effectively marking a false route away from the main force. The tactic worked well and although the Mosquitos were now being stalked by Luftwaffe night fighters, the performance of the British aircraft and crew were more than up to the job of outmanoeuvring the enemy.

Throughout September 1943, the Germans were well aware of how the Mosquito was being used by 8 Group. Because of the aircraft's habit of operating at higher altitudes, the enemy quickly developed flak which could burst at up to 30,000ft. Two of 139 Squadron's Mosquitos were coned over Dusseldorf and the subsequent barrage meant that each had to

return to England on a single engine. Sqn Ldr D A Braithwaite was coned over Brandenburg on September 14/15 en route to Berlin. The Mosquito was hit at least ten times by flak but, typifying the spirit of 139 Squadron, Braithwaite continued on to bomb Berlin and then returned home safely to Wyton.

By late October, Bennett found himself with a surplus of Mosquito crews which were more than sufficient to form a third flight for

modified but the centre of gravity, thanks to the extra weight, was causing a few headaches, and in the case of the Mosquito B.IV and B.IX, was never completely eradicated. Regardless of the CoG issues, a pair of modified B.IVs were delivered to Oakington for 627 Squadron but for some unknown reason were immediately transferred to Gravely for 692 Squadron. The two converted Mosquitos were ready for action and, on February 23, 1944, Sqn Ldr Watts and Fg Off C Hassell took off for Düsseldorf at 1903hrs. Right behind them was Flt Lt V S Moore and Plt Off P F Dillon, setting the stage

139 Squadron. However, he decided that the surplus would be best used to create a new unit. On November 12, 1943 eight crews were transferred from 139 Squadron to create 627 Squadron at Oakington.

The New Year brought another new unit to the 8 Group fold when 692 Squadron was formed at Gravely on January 1, 1944 under the command of Wg Cdr W G Lockhart. No 692 Squadron did not manage to contribute to the fight for most of January, but 139 and 627 Squadrons managed 184 successful sorties between them. One of these was an effective spoof on Berlin where TIs and Window were dropped causing the bulk of the German night fighter force to assemble over the capital while the main Allied force hit Stettin.

GH and H2S

By this time, 139 Squadron were being slowly steered towards becoming 8 Group's main marking squadron for the LNSF. Experiments with GH had been disappointing, but one Mosquito was modified to take H2S, and this flew operationally for the first time to Berlin on January 27/28. Five days later, the same aircraft led a small force of Mosquitos, including one from 692 Squadron on its first operation, on another raid to Berlin using H2S.

▲ An unidentified pilot and Wg Cdr W J R Shepherd OBE (right), 8 Group's Chief Intelligence Officer astride a 4,000lb 'Cookie' at Graveley. Mosquito DZ692 is behind in this photo taken in April 1944. *Via author*

Mosquito XX 'F' of 128 Squadron taxies for take-off at Wyton in late September 1944, not long after the unit had been re-formed. *Via author* ➤

The biggest raid of the war so far on Berlin on February 15/16 owed part of its success to Sqn Ldr S D Watts and an unwitting accomplice. Watts was busily laying a false route out of the target and, while checking to make sure his flares were being backed up, was amused and surprised to see a German aircraft reinforcing the flares behind him.

New weapons, tactics, techniques, and technology were continually being evaluated in order to more fully exploit the Mosquito's potential. A proposal was put forward in April 1943, suggesting the Mosquito was more than man enough to carry a bomb load of a single 4,000lb 'Cookie'. The bomb bay was easily

to see which crew would be the first drop a Cookie from a Mosquito. No 105 Squadron provided the small marking force, and, at 2045hrs, Watts' navigator/bomb aimer pressed the bomb release first and it was followed a minute later by the bomb from Moore's aircraft.

With only three squadrons making up 8 Group's LNSF, the Mosquitos still managed to fly 509 sorties of which 489 were successful. One successful spoof operation was flown by 627 Squadron on March 1/2. While the main force attacked Stuttgart, 11 Mosquitos created a complex diversion all the way to Munich, resulting in just four bombers being lost out of a force of 557 aircraft.

'A' Flight, 109 Squadron make time for a formal group photo at Little Staughton in October 1944. The squadron remained at the Cambridgeshire station until their disbandment on April 30, 1945. *Via author*

Mosquitos of 128 Squadron being waved off at dusk, for another operation from Wyton in late 1944. *Via author*

Growing in numbers

The LNSF continued to swell when 571 Squadron was formed at Downham Market on April 5, 1944. The squadron was initially to be a two-flight setup, but some of its intended aircraft were transferred to 105 Squadron which was now at Bourn. No 105 Squadron gained 'C' Flight as there was now a higher priority being placed on smaller targets within Oboe range and Bennett was well aware of the pressure being placed on his two Oboe-equipped squadrons.

No 571 Squadron took part in its first operation on April 12/13 when two crews were among 39 Mosquitos in an attack on Osnabrück. This size of raid was now becoming the norm for the LNSF and April 1944 in particular included some very large Mosquito raids. Thirty-five attacked Hannover at the beginning of the month, followed by 41 against Cologne and another 40 attacking Essen on April 8/9. The raid on April 13/14 saw Mosquitos carrying Cookies to Berlin for the first time. The extra fuel needed was carried in a pair of 50-gallon drop tanks which were neatly fitted under each wing.

On April 15, the LNSF shrank slightly when 627 Squadron was transferred to 5 Group to see the remainder of its wartime service out at Woodhall Spa. Despite the drop in manpower, the LNSF still managed to carry out 553 sorties with only the loss of a single aircraft.

As D-Day approached, Bomber Command were becoming increasingly pre-occupied with targets in Northern France. This did not stop the LNSF continuing to carry the fight to

Germany which included another seven attacks on Berlin. With still only three squadrons, the LNSF managed to fly 661 sorties but this figure would be on the rise again with the arrival of another squadron on August 1, 1944. No 608 Squadron was re-formed at Downham Market with the Mosquito B.XX and was destined to operate from the Norfolk airfield for the remainder of the war. Only four days later, Sqn Ldr J D Bolton flew the squadron's first operation to Wanne-Eickel. The squadron were in the thick of the action from the start and one very successful attack on Cologne on August 23/24 saw 'an enormous explosion lasting 45 seconds lit up streets and buildings'. It did not go all the LNSF's way that night though, with one 692 Squadron aircraft crashing en route, killing both crew, and Flt Lt S O Webb in 608 Squadron Mosquito B.XX KB242 being attacked at least four times by a night fighter. Webb and his navigator, Plt Off Campbell, were lucky to make it to Woodbridge uninjured.

The LNSF expanded again on September 5 when 128 Squadron joined the fold after re-forming at Wyton. Just five days later, the whole squadron joined the fight when it was part of a 47-strong force which attacked Berlin. The capital was attacked by the LNSF again the following night with another 47 Mosquitos led by 139 Squadron. However, it was not a good night for the Upwood-based unit which only managed to drop TIs from two of the nine aircraft designated. Enemy flak was also alarmingly accurate that night, resulting in the loss of Flt Lt J A F Halcro and Flt Lt T J Martin, both RCAF; their Mosquito crashing in the

Horst Wessel district of Berlin. Another 139 Squadron aircraft, flown by Plt Off H A Fawcett was hit by flak during his bombing run which knocked out an engine and damaged the hydraulics. Unable to open the bomb doors or lower its undercarriage, Mosquito B.XX KB227 limped back to Woodbridge where Fawcett executed a perfect crash landing with only minor injuries to himself and his navigator, Fg Off P L U Cross DFC.

With its Operation Overlord commitments declining, the heavy squadrons were now back in force against Germany and the LNSF were called upon to continue 'spoofing' and dropping Window on targets for 8 Group. Kiel and Frankfurt were among the targets attacked, with a raid on September 15/16 being particularly successful. While 490 aircraft attacked Kiel, nine Mosquitos 'spoofed' Lubeck with Window and TIs and followed this by bombing the port. Another 27 Mosquitos attacked Berlin and seven others 'windowed' Kiel in front of the main raid.

No 142 Squadron was the next unit to be reformed with Mosquito B.XXVs at Gransden Lodge on October 25. Two aircraft were part of a 59-strong Mosquito force targeting Cologne four days later and two more were over Berlin, joining 60 other Mosquitos in a two-phase diversion. Poor weather disrupted operations during November, but this did not stop the LNSF from attacking Hanover nine times in favour of Berlin. Thanks to the advancing allies, Oboe-guided raids could now be extended further east putting cities such as Stuttgart well within range. On November 5/6, 65 Mosquitos,

Long-serving Mosquito B.IV ML963 which first joined 8 Group with 109 Squadron, followed by 692 Squadron, before finally joining 571 Squadron not long after its formation at Oakington. The aircraft was abandoned on an operation to Berlin on April 10, 1945, both crew, Fg Off R D Oliver and Flt Sgt L M Young RAAF evaded capture. *Andy Hay/ww.flyingart.co.uk*

led by Oboe and backed up by 139 Squadron, hit the city in two phases 3 1/2 hours apart. Many of the crews involved, all of whom returned safely, reported huge fires and large explosions throughout both phases.

By early December, an average of over 60 Mosquitos were attacking main targets and this was set to increase, with the addition of another squadron on December 16, 1944. No 162 Squadron was re-formed at Bourn and along with several new crews for 139 Squadron were the first to be sent on 'Siren Tours' to gain H2S experience. These tours covered every corner of Germany and involved dropping a single 500lb bomb on three or four separate targets. While all crews benefitted from these long trips, it also resulted in keeping ground

LR503, 'F for Freddie' after completing its 203rd sortie, of an eventual 213, the last being flown to the rail yards at Leipzig on April 10, 1945. The Oboe-equipped Mosquitos of No's 105 and 109 Squadrons had their noses and side windows overpainted. *Howard Lees via author*

◄ A 4,000lb 'Cookie' is manoeuvred into position towards Mosquito VI PF432 of 128 Squadron at Wyton before an attack on Berlin on March 21, 1945. Having already served with 692 Squadron, PF432 was transferred to 180 and then 69 Squadron before being SOC at Wahn on August 5, 1947. *Via author*

defences on continuous alert and resulted in many lost man hours in the enemy factories without causing a great deal of damage. The first sirens were flown on December 23/24 against Bremen, Hanover, Münster, and Osnabrück. The same night, 52 Mosquitos attacked Limburg rail yards and another 40 attacked Siegburg while the heavies rested.

New Year's Day 1945 saw a classic example of the Mosquito in action when 17 of them attacked railway tunnels between the Rhine and the Ardennes battle area. The object of the exercise was to prevent German forces from being reinforced and in broad daylight and with

a 'cookie' apiece the Mosquitos dived to 200ft dropping their short-fuse delay bombs into the entrances of the tunnels. One crew, Plt D R Tucker and Sgt F A J David, of 571 Squadron, found three tunnels and after making a dummy run on each, in full view of the local villagers, dropped their cookie perfectly into the entrance. Tucker banked round to view his handy work and saw that the whole tunnel had erupted, causing the hillside to collapse into the path of an approaching train.

The final piece of the 8 Group Mosquito jigsaw was in place on January 25, 1945 when 163 Squadron was reformed at Wyton. This now meant that Bennett could muster

150 aircraft at a moment's notice without putting up a maximum effort.

The ever-increasing strength was put to good effect on February 1/2 when 176 Mosquito sorties were flown against eight separate targets. Ludwigshafen, Mainz, Siegen, Bruckhausen, Hanover, Nuremburg and Berlin were all hit; the latter involving 122 Mosquitos. Berlin would suffer mercilessly at the hands of the LNSF during the final months of the war and, from February 20/21, the capital was attacked on 36 consecutive nights. Averaging 60 Mosquitos per raid, 2,538 sorties were flown to Berlin of which 2,409 were successful. A devastating 855 cookies were dropped on the city during this period alone and the LNSF continued to bomb Berlin right up to arrival of the Russian forces in late April 1945.

The Mosquitos of 8 Group had performed exceptionally well and, since its formation, they had flown 28,215 sorties with the loss of just 100 aircraft (0.4%), 70 of which were lost by 139 Squadron alone. Approximately 26,000 tons of bombs, of which nearly 10,000 were cookies, were dropped on Germany; a remarkable achievement for a small, unarmed twin-engined bomber made of wood. ❧

◄ Approximately 10,000 'Cookies' were dropped on the enemy by 8 Group's LNSF. This crew and ground crew of a 608 Squadron Mosquito at Downham Market, prepare to drop their last on Kiel on May 2/3, 1945. Note the 635 Squadron codes 'F2-D' on the bomb trolley; this Lancaster's war was by then already over. *Via author*

BAY 3
WEEKLY PRODUCTION
of MOSQUITOS
THIS WEEKS OBJECTIVE — 10
PRODUCTION TO DATE — 4
QUOTA

The de Havilland Canada Mosquito production in Toronto on March 13, 1944. 1,134 Mosquitoes were built in Canada, the vast majority during the Second World War. *Joe Holliday via Aeroplane*

A very atmospheric and dramatic shot of a 464 Squadron Mosquito FB.VI snapped by a resident of Copenhagen during the Operation *Carthage* raid on March 21, 1945. *Via Martyn Chorlton*

Operation *Carthage*

The raid was right out of the pages of *Boy's Own* magazine and is still discussed today, as François Prins relates.

A trio of Mosquito FB.VIs carry out high-level formation practice over their home airfield at B 87/ Rosières-en-Santerre, 18 miles west of Amiens, prior to the Copenhagen raid. *Via Martyn Chorlton*

Under occupation

Only those who have lived in a country that has been invaded by an enemy can understand the grief and horror that comes with an occupying force. Nazi Germany moved swiftly through France to capture the Low Countries as well as Norway and Denmark. Resistance against the enemy was strong and widespread throughout the occupied territories and those who waged an unceasing war against the oppressors did so with great courage. They knew that they were at risk at all times and they also knew that they were at the mercy of traitors who had been coerced by the enemy. None of us can say how

we would react unless we are placed in the position that was endured by those who lived under the Nazi occupation. Speaking to those who survived is always a rewarding and humbling experience.

On April 9, 1940, Nazi troops over-ran Denmark and an ultimatum was delivered: if Denmark offered no resistance, Germany would respect Danish political independence. The Danish government and monarch – King Christian X - had no option but to agree. Denmark is a country with a small population and stood no chance when the Nazi forces arrived. Interestingly, Denmark was in a peculiar

position as it was technically neutral, neither at war with Germany nor allied to her. The King continued to reign and his ministers to govern in parliament. That did not mean that the Nazis were not regarded as the enemy and from early on the Danes were in contact with the Special Operations Executive in London.

Growing resistance

Resistance to the invader was strong and never let up in the five years of occupation. To show their solidarity, the Danes took to wearing four coins tied together with red and white ribbons in their buttonholes. Red and

Sqn Ldr A F Carlisle and Flt Lt N J Ingram in Mosquito FB.VI, PZ306 pictured whilst practising low flying for Operation *Carthage*. PZ306 only served with 21 Squadron and remained on strength until November 23, 1946. *Via Martyn Chorlton*

Mosquito FB.VI SZ977 of 21 Squadron as flown by Wg Cdr P A Kleboe DSO, DFC, AFC and his navigator, Fg Off K Hall. *Andy Hay/www.flyingart.co.uk*

white are the Danish colours and four coins totalled nine Ore representing the date of the occupation, April 9. Initially, unlike other conquered European countries, the Jews in Denmark were not compelled to wear a yellow Star of David and, although registered, were not selected for transportation to concentration camps.

To combat the enemy, the Danes set up a seven-man Freedom Council to lead the resistance groups which blew up factories that worked for Nazi Germany, destroyed or damaged railway tracks, bridges, military facilities, oil and petrol tanks. Their main weapon was sabotage and generally not accepting the fact that they were under Nazi

An expert at planning low-level attacks with the Mosquito, Air Vice-Marshal Basil Embry, (second left) briefs senior officers. To Embry's right is Air Commodore David Atcherley, to his left is Group Captain Peter Wykeham-Barnes and Wing Commander Pat Shallard. *Via Martyn Chorlton* ➤

A very rare and possibly the only image in existence of the Mosquito force of Operation *Carthage* departing Fersfield in Norfolk on the morning of March 21, 1945. This is one of the six Mosquitoes of 21 Squadron setting out for Copenhagen. *Via Martyn Chorlton*

rule; Danes even rioted in the streets during the occupation. In its fight, Denmark was greatly assisted by neutral Sweden which acted as a halfway house for supplies from Britain. The Swedish authorities could not openly support weapons being sent to Denmark but many Swedish customs officers and policemen turned a blind-eye to shipments that landed at a Swedish port for onward transport to Denmark.

Like some other occupied countries, the Danes defied their oppressors with a series of strikes. In the summer of 1943 they took their strike action, coupled with resistance activities and an illegal press, to a new height. This resulted in Hitler demanding that the Danish government declare a state of emergency; they refused to comply and resigned in protest. Hitler ordered the German commander-in-chief, Hermann von Hanneken, to impose martial law and to arrest and deport the Danish Jews. On October 2, 1943, the order went out to round up the Jews but by then nearly all of the Jews in Copenhagen had already been warned and gone into hiding while government officials secretly negotiated an agreement with Sweden to receive them. Only 284 of an estimated 7,000 Jews in the area were rounded up and over the coming weeks most of them made their way to Sweden on fishing boats, private vessels and any other type of floating craft that could undertake the journey. Fewer than 500 Danish Jews were deported to the Theresienstadt concentration camp in Czechoslovakia, and

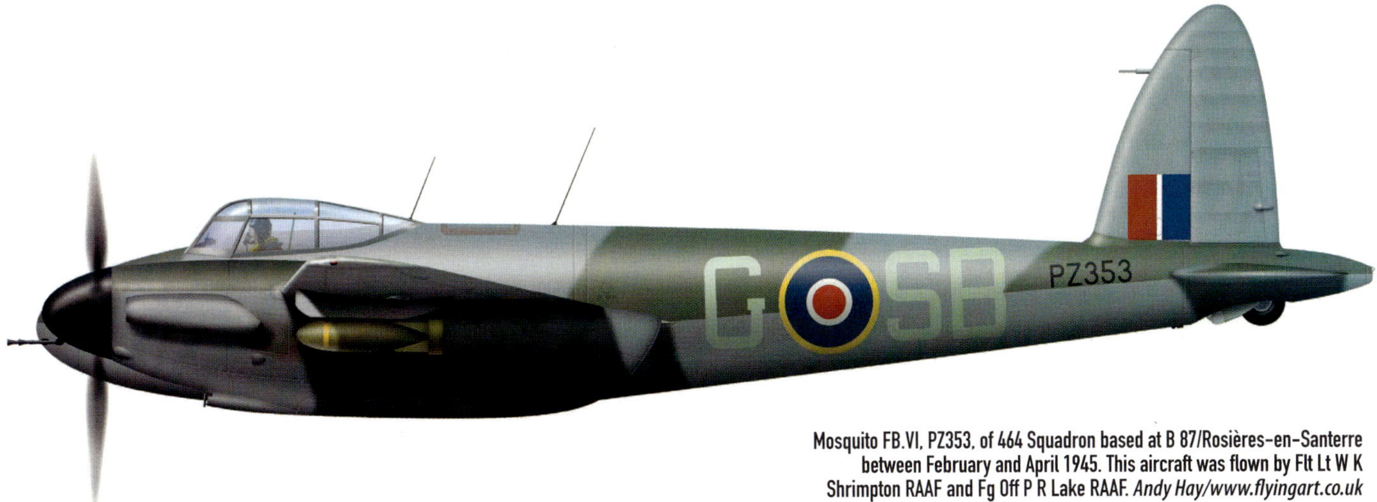

Mosquito FB.VI, PZ353, of 464 Squadron based at B 87/Rosières-en-Santerre between February and April 1945. This aircraft was flown by Flt Lt W K Shrimpton RAAF and Fg Off P R Lake RAAF. *Andy Hay/www.flyingart.co.uk*

nearly 90 per cent of them survived to return to Denmark after the war.

The Danish people all regarded themselves as being in The Resistance and life was never easy for the Nazi occupiers, they were continually harassed and exasperated by a well-organised underground movement. Britain supplied the needs of the Danish fighters with a regular service between the two countries by air and sea. However, the Gestapo were getting more active and, to destroy records held at their offices in Aarhus, an RAF raid was mounted on October 31, 1944. Mosquitoes successfully bombed the building and killed several of the enemy as well as destroying their vital records.

The Freedom Council takes charge

This did not deter the enemy and they turned their attentions to the Freedom Council and the resistance; they started to arrest leaders of the group. By the end of the year, the Gestapo had rounded up 26 senior members of The Resistance and imprisoned them at their Copenhagen headquarters, the building which, in peacetime, had been the head office of the Shell Oil Company. It was imperative that the Danes be freed or killed before they were tortured to reveal any secrets.

Through their network, the banned Freedom Council heard that the Gestapo were planning to arrest more of their number. One of the leading members of the Freedom Council who had evaded capture was Ole Lippmann. He acted as liaison officer between the Danish resistance and the allies, and requested that the RAF attack the Gestapo headquarters in an air raid that ended up being the deadliest wartime operation in Denmark. In a later interview with the Berlingske Tidende newspaper, Lippman said that the raid was a terrible decision to make because he knew civilian casualties were likely but that it was the right decision.

Although the raid on Aarhus had been a success, Britain initially turned down the Copenhagen request as too risky, due to the location in a crowded city centre and the need for low-level bombing but, eventually, after repeated requests, the raid was approved. Once approval had been given, planning commenced but took several weeks. Group Captain (later Air-Vice Marshal) Basil Embry had led the RAF team who had planned the Aarhus raid and was tasked with the new mission which was given the codename Operation *Carthage*.

Embry was a highly experienced pilot who had been shot down over enemy territory and successfully escaped to return to Britain and active service. He planned the raid in great detail with scale models of the target building and the city itself. He knew that if it were to succeed the raid would have to be made at very-low level and take the enemy by surprise. The only aircraft that could be considered for the mission was the Mosquito.

A force is despatched

With plans in place, Operation *Carthage* was given the go-ahead for March 21, 1945. At 0855hrs, 20 Mosquitos of 21, 464 and 487 Squadrons from 140 Wing, 2 (Bomber) Group, escorted by 30 Mustang Mk IIIs from 64, 126 and 234 Squadrons, took off from Fersfield in Norfolk. 18 of the bombers were Mosquito FB. VIs and two were Mosquito B.IVs from the RAF Film Production Unit (FPU). They filmed the flight from Britain to Denmark and the attack on the Shellhus. The Mosquito bombers carried a total of 44 500lb bombs. Three Mustangs turned back with problems shortly after take-off.

Following take-off from Fersfield, the aircraft flew in a loose formation across the North Sea and, on arrival at Tissoe, a lake in western Zeeland, they split into three waves. The first comprised seven Mosquitos (one FPU) and twelve Mustangs: the second six Mosquitos and the third seven Mosquitos (one FPU), with Mustangs split between them. To maximise the element of surprise, the plan was that the three formations would take different routes to Copenhagen but then adjust their heading so that they would all approach Copenhagen from the south-west. The aircraft were expected to head for the town of Koge, about 20 miles south of the capital, and then turn to follow the coastline to Avedoere from where they would turn north towards the landmark Carlsberg brewery, passing it on the eastern side. Their last point of reference was the 'Det Ny Teater', a theatre on the south-eastern corner of the most southern of the four lakes. From the theatre, the

◄ Eight 500lb bombs were dropped directly onto the intended target, the HQ of the local Gestapo at the Shellhus, pictured in the left half of this low-level strike photo. *Via Martyn Chorlton*

The raid on the Shellhus was led by Wg Cdr R N Bateson and Sqn Ldr E B Sismore in their 487 Squadron, Mosquito FB.VI, RS570.
Andy Hay/www.flyingart.co.uk

aircraft would be able to see the landmarks such as the Town Hall, as depicted in the models they had studied and attack the Shellhus - located on the north side of Kampmandsgade between Nyrupsgade and Vester Farimagsgade - from the south. That was the plan.

The Mustangs, which escorted the bombers on both outward and return journeys and during the actual attack, were tasked with dealing with the various anti-aircraft gun positions in the vicinity. However, the raid was a complete surprise and caught the enemy gunners out. They did not fire on the attacking force until they had completed the bombing raid and turned for home. Some flak-ships in the harbour fired on the bombers as they flew overhead.

It was only the first wave that followed the planned approach. The two following waves took a more direct course to Copenhagen. The third wave came in from the west instead of the south.

Tragedy in Frederiksberg

When the first wave passed the railway goods yard, one of the Mosquitos hit a tall mast or post and crashed behind the Institut Jeanne d'Arc, a Roman Catholic school in Frederiksberg Allé, Frederiksberg. The rest of the wave found and bombed the target. However, the fire and smoke from the crashed Mosquito was mistaken for the target by the next wave of aircraft which dropped their bombs on and around the crash site.

The resulting fires soon spread to other buildings and eventually engulfed the school, which burned to the ground in less than two hours. 86 children and ten teachers lost their lives in this tragedy and 67 were injured. When rescuers reached the school cellars, they found the bodies of 42 children huddled together. All had drowned in water from the firemen's hoses. It was a great tragedy and one that is all too common in war.

Not all of the second wave aircraft were confused by the smoke and flames and realized their mistake before they bombed and so turned toward the Shellhus, but only one of the aircraft was able to bomb the target. The third wave approached Copenhagen from the west and all but one of the aircraft in this wave dropped their bombs on the French school.

Bombing the Shellhus

Meanwhile, the Shellhus was hit by eight 500lb bombs, six in the western wing, towards Nyropsgade, and two in the eastern wing, towards Vester Farimagsgade. The west wing collapsed and a fire started. It was a windy day and the fire quickly spread, burning it down.

Intelligence had informed the RAF that the prisoners were held on the top floor of the building in make-shift cells. These cells had been built to minimize transportation of prisoners from the Vestre Faengsel prison in Copenhagen for interrogation and torture in the Shellhus. To avoid hitting the cell-block floor, bombs were fitted with delayed fuses and were aimed at the lower parts of the building. Six bombs exploded in the western wing, where nine prisoners were being held; six were killed instantaneously and one died when he jumped from the fifth floor to the ground. All 14 prisoners in the southern wing survived as no bombs hit this part of the building. Three prisoners were being interrogated on the fifth floor and one died. There were no prisoners in the eastern wing. The Germans played down their casualties but around 55 Germans and 47 Danes who worked for the Gestapo were killed. Some accounts put the number of Gestapo

Another dramatic shot of one of the escorting Mustang IIIs caught low over Copenhagen on March 21, 1945.
Via Martyn Chorlton

▲ A poignant memorial to the 86 children and ten teachers who lost their lives in the Jeanne d'Arc School in Frederiksburg. Copenhagen. *Via Owen Cooper*

Above the aircrew plaque, a propeller blade on the side of the Shell building also commemorates Operation *Carthage*. *Via Owen Cooper*

killed at twice that number. The enemy stated at the time that none of the Gestapo had been in the building when the attack took place, which was clearly not true. The attack has always been seen as a success because of the many surviving prisoners – 18 out of 26 – but it could have been worse. Operation *Carthage* helped to thwart the Gestapo's arrest plans in Denmark.

Aftermath

A reconnaissance aircraft took off the following day and photographed the objective. These photographs showed that the target had received severe damage. The top storey and roof of the south front were destroyed and the remainder was partially gutted and destroyed. The west wing was destroyed nearly to ground level and the east wing, the top storey and roof were destroyed and the floor below damaged. A photograph received later from Danish sources showed the building ablaze.

Basil Embry later wrote: 'I discussed the possibilities of Danish casualties with Major Truelson who was temporarily attached to my headquarters while we were planning the operation. He assured me that they would sooner die from our bombing than at the hands of the Germans, adding, "Who knows, some might not be killed and succeed in escaping, as happened at Aarhus, and anyhow their death will save many more Danish lives, so don't worry." We succeeded in destroying Gestapo records and liberating the prisoners. It will always remain a miracle to me that anyone inside the building survived to tell the tale.'

Of the 20 Mosquitos taking part in the attack, 16 returned. One had crashed in the goods yard behind the school before bombing and three more were shot down off the coast of northern Zeeland after the attack. One Mustang crashed in a park north of the Shellhus. The primary objective for the fighters was to attack anti-aircraft gun positions in central Copenhagen. Nine RAF pilots and crew were killed in the attack. Three are buried at Bispebjerg kirkegaard, the remaining six crashed over the sea and were never found.

After the war, Shell Denmark returned to their head office and to mark the famous raid they had mounted on the wall of the building a bronze-cast of a propeller from one of the crashed Mosquito bombers. Below the propeller is a plaque with the names of the RAF crew members who were killed in the attack. In Copenhagen, the Museum of Resistance (Frihedsmuseet) has on display one of the models of the city that was built and used by the RAF when they planned the attack. ❖

A memorial to the nine airmen who failed to return from Operation *Carthage* on the outside of the Shell building in Copenhagen. The eulogy says 'Fight for all that you hold dear, die if you so must, life is then less hard to bear, and death its sting has lost.' *Via Owen Cooper* ▼

CREWS, UNITS AND AIRCRAFT THAT TOOK PART IN OPERATION *CARTHAGE*, MARCH 21, 1945

*21 Squadron**
SZ977   Wg Cdr P A Kleboe & Fg Off K Hall (crashed on garage in Frederiksburg)
PZ306   Sqn A F Carlisle & Flt Lt N J Ingram
LR388   Sqn Ldr A C Henderson & Flt Lt W A Moore
HR162   Flt Lt M Hetherington & Fg Off J K Bell
*Two other aircraft were involved but are not listed in squadron records
464 Squadron
PZ353   Flt Lt W K Shrimpton RAAF & Fg Off P R Lake RAAF
PZ463   Flt Lt C B Thompson & Sgt H D Carter
PZ309   Flt Lt A J Smith RAAF & Flt Sgt H L Green RAAF
SZ999   Fg Off R G Dawson RAAF & Fg Off F T Murray (missing)
RS609   Fg Off J H Palmer RAAF & Sub Lt H H Becker RNorgeN (missing)
SZ968   Wg Cdr Iredale RAAF & Fg Off Johnson
487 Squadron
RS570   Wg Cdr R N Bateson & Sqn Ldr E B Sismore
PZ402   Wg Cdr F M Denton & Fg Off A J Coe (damaged by flak, SOC on return)
PZ462   Flt Lt R J Dempsey & Flt Sgt E J Paige
PZ339   Sqn Ldr W P Kemp & Flt Lt R Peel
SZ985   Fg Off G L Peet & Fg Off L A Graham
NT123   Flt Lt D V Pattison & Flt Sgt F Pygram (missing)
FPU
Two unidentified Mosquito B.IVs
64, 126 & 234 Squadrons
30 Mustang IIIs (one aircraft lost, Flt Lt D A Drew (64 Sqn) killed)

Nicknamed 'Tsetse', the Mosquito FB.XVIII was a development from the FB.VI with the nose modified to take a six-pounder (57mm) anti-tank gun. Only 20 examples of this formidable aircraft were built, virtually all of them seeing action over the North Sea and off the Norwegian Coast as part of the Strike Wings. *Aeroplane*

The Banff Strike Wing

Martyn Chorlton provides a brief history of the activities of a few heavily armed Mosquitos which wreaked havoc off the Norwegian coast during the final months of World War Two

A new strike wing

By mid-1944, plans were already afoot to move the Coastal Command Mosquito and Beaufighter strike wings to the northeast of Scotland. The decision was taken as a direct result of the withdrawal of U-boats from the west coast of France to bases in Germany and Scandinavia.

On September 1, 1944, Banff was taken over by 18 Group Coastal Command which controlled a mixed strike wing made up of 144 and 404 Squadron Beaufighters and 235 Squadron operating the Mosquito FB.VI. The group also controlled a second Mosquito strike wing consisting of 248 Squadron and 333 (Norwegian) Squadron. The entire wing was under the command of Gp Capt J W M 'Max' Aitken DSO, DFC.

It was the Norwegian-crewed Mosquito FB.VIs of 'B' Flight, 333 Squadron which were the first 'armed' aircraft to arrive. No 333 Squadron's main task while serving in the strike wing was reconnaissance operations along the Norwegian coast and their first sortie from Banff took place on September 2. Their local knowledge was invaluable and, as the operations gained momentum, the squadron would also act as Pathfinders on many occasions, leading the main force into the attack.

Nos 144 and 404 (RCAF) 'Buffalo' Squadrons arrived from Strubby on September 3, both equipped with the Beaufighter TF.X. Both squadrons were in the air on September 6, contributing 26 aircraft for a shipping strike. Frustratingly, the operation was abandoned

due to bad weather but, by the time the Beaufighters had returned, another squadron had arrived to bolster the strength of the strike wing. No 235 Squadron, equipped with the Mosquito FB.VI, arrived from Portreath to provide fighter protection for the two Beaufighter squadrons. And, by the time 235 Squadron returned to Banff after completing its first operation, 248 Squadron also arrived from Portreath with its Mosquitos. Among 248 Squadron's assets was a handful of Mosquito FB.XVIIIs fitted with the 57mm Molins 6lb Class M nose cannon.

Rovers off the Norwegian coast

A typical raid took place on September 14, when all four squadrons were airborne on a *Rover*-armed reconnaissance patrol

Colin Doggett captures the dramatic few seconds' worth of intense action during a 143 Squadron Mosquito attack on merchant vessels in a Norwegian Fjord in early 1945. *Colin Doggett*

Mosquito FB.VI RF610 of 248 Squadron captured off the Scottish coast. This aircraft survived the war and ended its days serving with the Yugoslavian Air Force. *Via author*

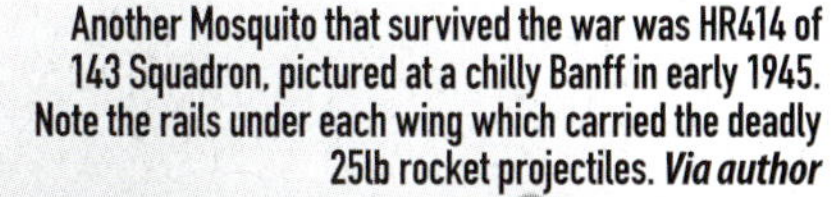

Another Mosquito that survived the war was HR414 of 143 Squadron, pictured at a chilly Banff in early 1945. Note the rails under each wing which carried the deadly 25lb rocket projectiles. *Via author*

On arrival at Banff, 248 Squadron were equipped with the Mosquito FB.XVIII which carried a weapon unique to Coastal Command. Just under the nose of the Mosquito can be seen a 57mm 6lb Class M cannon more familiarly known as the Molins gun. Nicknamed 'Tsetse' only 27 ever served with the RAF. *Via author*

off Norway. Twenty-five Mosquitos were contributed by 235 and 248 Squadrons, while 144 and 404 despatched 19 Beaufighters between them. While approaching Kristiansund, four enemy merchant vessels (MV) were spotted with two escorts, the German auxiliary trawler *Sulldorf* and the *Innsbruck*. The aircraft quickly swung into action and, on the first pass, several MVs were hit, including the *Pompeji* and the *Iris* which was seriously damaged by at least 22 rocket hits. The escorts put up a ferocious barrage of flak, but it was not enough to stop the *Sulldorf* from being sunk. It was not all one way though, one 404 Squadron Beaufighter had to ditch in the sea, and another was damaged by flak and had to make the 500 mile return trip to Banff on a single engine.

Three more merchant vessels were claimed sunk during operations on September 21 and 24. The *Vangsnes* and *Hygia* were sunk at Lister and the *Biber* off Hjeltefjord. Accurate flak over the latter saw one 248 Squadron Mosquito return to base with a large part of the leading edge of its wing missing.

Detachments from 281 Squadron, flying Vickers Warwicks on Air Sea Rescue duties, had been operating in the area since March 1944 and would continue to do so until the end of the war. On October 22, 404 Squadron made the short flight to Dallachy, followed the next day by 144 Squadron. The same day, 143 Squadron arrived from North Coates with their Mosquitos having only just converted from the Beaufighter.

No 235 Squadron had not even seen an enemy aircraft since August 9. This was about to change when elements of the Luftwaffe's IV/ZG26, equipped with the Bf110, moved from Ørlandet to bolster the unit at Fliergerhorst Herdla and began to intercept long-range shipping patrols. To meet this problem, 18 Group instructed two 235 Squadron Mosquitos to fly a *Rover* patrol from Marstein to Stadlandet on October 24 in the hope of turning the tables on the German fighters. Four Bf110s were intercepted west of Bergen and within minutes three of them were diving in flames towards the sea.

The wing grows

No 143 Squadron flew its first operational sortie with the Mosquito on November 7,

Armourers hard at work, loading RPs onto Mosquito FB.VI PZ438, at Banff in February 1945. This aircraft was brought down by flak over Ålesund on March 17, 1945. *Via author*

was another 143 Squadron Mosquito, shot down by a Bf109.

The strike wing returned to Leirvik harbour on January 15, 1945 with 16 Mosquitos of 143, 235, 248 and a pair from 333 Squadron taking part. The weather was atrocious from the outset and the small force had to fly so low over the sea that their propellers left a wake behind them. The force was on the hunt for the *Claus Rickmers* which was believed to carrying 'heavy water' in connection with the German attempt to produce an atomic bomb. The target was found in the harbour along with several MVs and flak ships plus a large number of anti-aircraft guns. Despite the hail of anti-aircraft fire the attackers faced, the strike wing still managed to sink two MVs and a trawler but despite being hit by everything the Mosquito had, the *Claus Rickmers* would not sink. One

but poor weather disrupted further flying until November 13. On this day, 235 and 248 Squadrons, along with 144 and 489 Squadron's Beaufighters attacked shipping off Egersund, west of Rekefjord leaving one MV damaged and two smaller vessels sunk.

Another operation had mixed results on December 16. Twenty-two Mosquitos took off from 0946hrs, although one had to make an emergency landing owing to the failure of a constant speed unit. A single 333 Squadron Mosquito led the force towards the already crippled MV *Ferndale* and the Norwegian salvage tug *Parat* in the narrow sound at Kraakbellesund. The MV was left in flames and a small flak vessel was sunk at the expense of a pair of Mosquitos.

Boxing Day 1944 was celebrated with a combined Banff/Dallachy operation after several tempting shipping targets had been spotted at Leirvik by a 333 Squadron crew. No 143 Squadron led the attack which concentrated on the steamer *Cygnus* and MV *Tenerife*, the latter carrying a cargo of pyrite. Tsetse rounds and rockets rained down on the vessels which were left burning and smoking.

Another successful strike, on December 28, sunk the 617 ton MV *La France* in Skudesnes without loss and further success was achieved on December 31 when three MVs were sunk in Flekkerfjord.

Fifteen Banff Mosquitos joined 21 Dallachy-based Beaufighters on an armed

One of two ships that were sunk during the successful strike on shipping at Sandefjord on April 2, 1945. This Mosquito has already launched its RPs and can be seen firing its cannon at the vessel below the water line. *Via author*

strike to Flekkerfjord on January 11. As the force prepared to attack, they were met not only with intense and accurate flak, but also the Lista-based Bf109s and Fw190s of JG5. RPs were jettisoned and the more manoeuvrable Mosquitos took on the fighters while trying to protect the escaping Beaufighters. At least four enemy fighters were shot down, two of them claimed by Flt Lt N Russell of 235 Squadron. Two aircraft failed to return, the first belonged to Flt Sgt P Smoolenaers of 143 Squadron, who flew into the sea trying to shake off an enemy fighter. The second loss

333 Squadron Mosquito was shot down as it approached the harbour and a 235 Squadron Mosquito had to crash land after being hit during the attack, killing the pilot. After surviving the onslaught over the harbour, the force had been briefed to leave via the quickest route possible which was also the most dangerous owing to the proximity of the Fw190s of 9 Staffel based at Herdla. Most of the crews ignored the brief but, of those who didn't, four more aircraft were shot down making this the worst day of the war so far for the Banff strike wing.

FB.VI RF610 of 248 Squadron survived the war after seeing constant action with the Banff strike wing was transferred to APS Acklington then 1 OFU before seeing out its days with the Yugoslavian Air Force as '8114'. *Andy Hay/www.flyingart.co.uk*

▲ A Mosquito FB.VI of 235 Squadron has its engines run up on the edge of Banff in early 1945 with the North Sea providing a backdrop. *Via author*

◄ The peace and tranquility of Porsgrunn was shattered as the Banff strike wing wreaks havoc amongst the Merchant Vessels moored there. Four were sunk and two damaged before the formation was pounced on by German fighters only minutes after this photo was taken. One 333 Squadron Mosquito failed to return. *Via author*

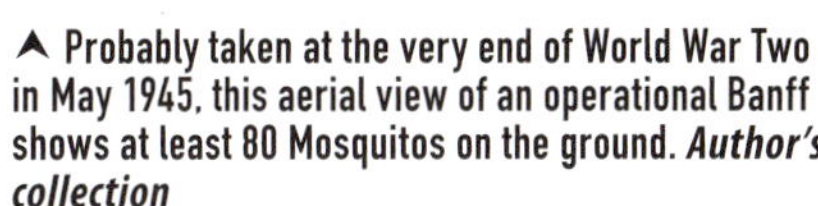

▲ Probably taken at the very end of World War Two in May 1945, this aerial view of an operational Banff shows at least 80 Mosquitos on the ground. *Author's collection*

Fighter escort all the way

Poor weather disrupted operations throughout January and February but this did not stop a Banff wing sortie on February 3 involving 143, 235 and 248 Squadrons. Seventeen Mosquitos, with a 65 Squadron Mustang escort, headed for Bergen to attack shipping. While southeast of Ålesund, Bf109s and Fw190s of 10/JG5 were spotted, the latter acting as top cover. The Bf109s went straight for the Mosquitos but were quickly intercepted by the Mustangs who later claimed three enemy fighters destroyed without loss to the RAF.

The weather continued to hamper operations, with many sorties flown, but all were aborted and the sight of Mosquitos returning to Banff with their RPs still onboard was becoming disconcerting. It was not until February 21 that 15 Mosquitos, all from 235 Squadron were joined by 65 Squadron, before the small force set off for Norway again. After spotting three MVs through a gap in the clouds near Leirvik, the Mosquitos swooped down and within minutes one was sunk and two were seriously damaged.

Ålesund was notorious for being the most heavily defended port in Norway but this did not deter a force of 31 Mosquitos setting out to attack it on March 17, 1945. Surrounded by four coastal batteries and a multitude of flak and machine-gun emplacements, a warm welcome was guaranteed for the attackers. A 333 Squadron outrider reported to the main force following that seven merchant vessels were at anchor in the port and the weather was good enough to carry out an attack. The defenders would certainly have spotted the 333 Squadron Mosquito and were ready for the inevitable attack to follow. Knowing this, the main force headed inland and approached Ålesund from the east in an effort to catch the defences off guard. The different approach worked and, within minutes of the attack beginning, three MVs were sunk, and two others were damaged.

No let up

While the war in mainland Europe was steadily coming to an end, the pace at Banff seemed to increase as strikes became bigger and ever more successful but losses were still mounting. Another 42 Mosquitos with 12 Mustangs as escort set out for Stadlandet, Aslesund and Dalsfjord which were all heavily defended areas. On approaching the Norwegian coast, the strike wing split into two formations, one of which was led by Sqn Ldr R Reid of 235 Squadron who on arrival over the target, led the force towards a large German MV moored

All is calm, all is quiet; the war is over for the strike wing Mosquitos at Banff all assembled in preparation for disbandment. *Flight via Aeroplane* ▼

Mosquito FB.VI PZ438 of 143 Squadron which was shot down by flak over Leirvik on January 15, 1945 whilst attacking the *Claus Rickmers. Andy Hay/www.flyingart.co.uk*

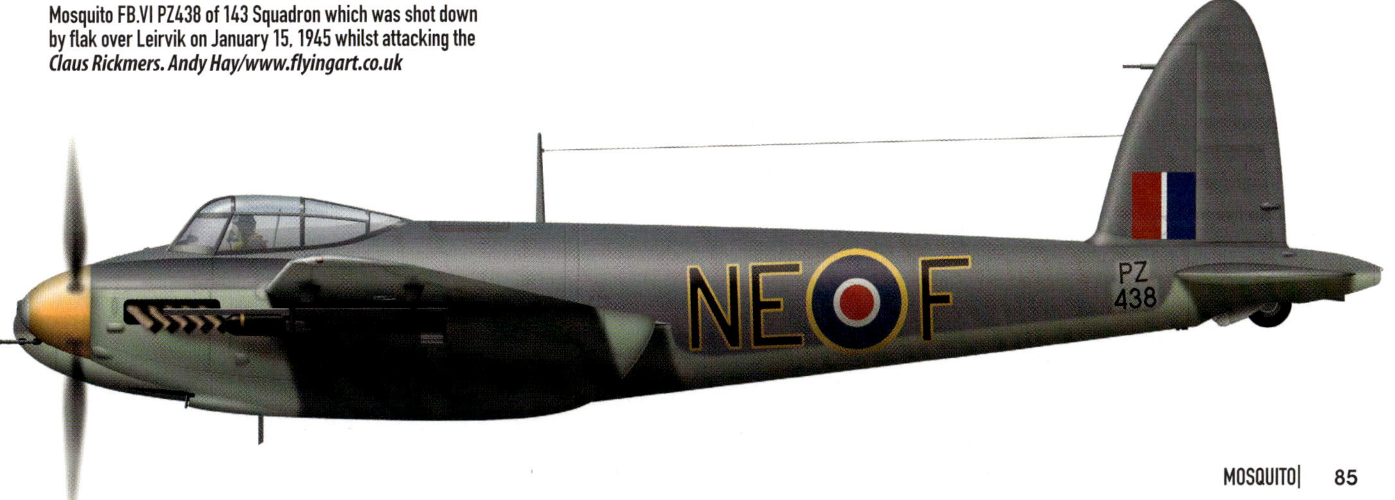

empty-handed, but the 15 Mosquitos led by Foxley-Norris managed to attack the MV which was left taking on water. Several other MVs were damaged during the day's operation but four Mosquitos failed to return, only one of their crews surviving to become POWs.

By April, the Germans were running out of serviceable dry docks in which to repair the increasing number of damaged ships. The only serious location available was Sanderfjord and this was one of several potential targets that received a reconnaissance flight in the early hours of April 2. The Famnaes shipyard was to be the focus of 36 RP-loaded Mosquitos which left at 1400hrs, accompanied by 65 Squadron. Ahead of the force, a 333 Squadron crew spotted nine MVs at the shipyard including the German 6,031 ton *Kattegat* which was conveniently being repaired in the dry dock. As the attack began, it was the *Kattegat* that bore the brunt of the first wave which hit the vessel at least 30 times with RPs severely damaging it. In the harbour, MVs undergoing repairs were sunk, including the 5,154 ton *Concordia* and the *William Blumer* which both succumbed to RP strikes. Three others were left severely damaged and in flames as the force set course for home without losing a single aircraft.

The wing is complete

Banff gained a fifth Mosquito squadron when 404 (Buffalo) Squadron returned from Dallachy to re-equip with the Mosquito. This long-serving squadron had been flying the Beaufighter since September 1942 and had been achieving success while serving from Dallachy. Its conversion to the new aircraft was swift and within three weeks the Canadians were ready for operations.

At Banff, all talk was of U-boats and intelligence accurately reported that 70 such vessels were travelling through the Kattegat and Skagerrak en route to Norwegian bases. This mass move was caused by the rapid advance of the Soviet forces, forcing the U-boats to hastily give up their Baltic homes. A plan was quickly formulated and, despite a poor weather report from an earlier meteorological flight, a force of 31 Mosquitos, loaded with drop tanks and RPs, set off for the Kattegat. By the time the force arrived over the target, the weather improved, and it was not long before two wakes were spotted on the surface. By the end of the attacks, U-*804*, U-*843* and U-*1065* had been sunk for the loss of one Mosquito which had been brought down by one of the exploding submarines.

More success followed on April 11, when all of Banff's squadrons set out for Porsgrunn again. The defending flak was very light, and the Mosquitos had another field day sinking three Norwegian MVs. A single German MV *Kalmar* was also sunk. Two further vessels were damaged as the force turned for home only to be taken by surprise as the Bf109s of 16./JG5 made a determined attack. The force had to fly at tree top level with their throttles wide open for over 20 minutes before the first dogfights ensued. One 333 Squadron Mosquito was brought down by the enemy fighters. Flt Lt

at the southern end of the Dalsfjord. The MV was loaded with ammunition and was not only protected by a flak ship, but also by the many gun positions on the shore line. As Reid dived to mast top height, his Mosquito suffered a direct hit, exploded, and crashed 50 yards beyond the MV. This did not save the vessel as the main force relentlessly hit the ship leaving it in flames with many casualties onboard. The second formation, led by Wg Cdr C Foxley-Norris, split again, with one group heading for Sandshamn and the other led by Sqn Ldr Robinson, to Måloy. The latter group returned

P Davenport and his navigator, Fg Off R Day, in their 235 Squadron Mosquito had been hit during their RP attack and, rather than trying to bale out he decided to switch off both engines and make a force landing on the frozen Langen Lake. They both survived to spend the final few weeks of the war in captivity.

Mopping up the U-boats

The regularity of attacks from Banff did not relent and U-boats were on the agenda again on April 19 when 22 Mosquitos headed for the Kattegat with the usual Mustang escort. Four U-boats led by a German minesweeper were spotted on the surface en route to Horten. As the attack began, the lead U-boat managed to crash-dive in time and escape but U-251 and U-2335 received the brunt of the attack and damaged U-2502. U-251, after being hit by at least 24 rockets, was sunk while the remainder managed to limp into various ports for repairs.

At this late stage of the war, it not only seems remarkable but potentially suicidal for the Luftwaffe to launch an attack against a convoy off the Scottish coast. But this is exactly what was expected of the crews of 6.KG26 flying the Ju88A-17 and 7./KG26, operating the Ju188A-3, from the nearest airfield to Scotland at Stavanger-Sola. The 12 Ju88s and six Ju188s were tasked to carry out armed sweeps along the northeast Scottish coast. As the small force set out from its Norwegian base, a larger force of 42 Mosquitos escorted by 24 Mustangs set course for the Kattegat in the hope of finding more targets. The force only found an endless blanket of thick mist which made any kind shipping strike virtually impossible. The order was given set course for home and the escorting Mustangs, who had a party to get back for at Peterhead, were given permission to open the throttles and go on ahead. Unfortunately for the enemy bombers, which had unsuccessfully completed their sweep for coastal shipping, they set course directly into the path of the fully armed Mosquitos. Foxley-Norris gave the order to attack, and all 42 Mosquitos dived down on the 18 enemy aircraft which were hugging the waves, oblivious of what was about to be unleashed upon them. The onslaught left an impression of the sea being on fire as, in quick succession nine enemy aircraft were shot down and all who managed to escape were damaged in some shape or form. While some return fire was received, no Mosquitos were lost and on return, the mood was jubilant and the biggest party the airfield had seen continued through to the following morning.

The final operation of the war from Banff took place on May 4. Once again led by Wg Cdr Foxley-Norris, it involved all five operational squadrons totalling 48 Mosquitos plus 18 Mustangs from 19 and 234 Squadrons with a pair of Fraserburgh-based Warwicks in ASR support. En route, a single E-boat was caught

in the open water off the Danish coast, and this was quickly sunk in an attack by 333 and 404 Squadron. As the large force approached Kiel, four destroyers were spotted, but as the force headed for them, Foxley-Norris's navigator saw two large MVs, a pair of frigates and a flak ship in convoy east of Aarhus Bay. The formation, with Foxley-Norris in the lead, prepared itself to attack the convoy. The Mosquitos hit a MV loaded with food and 700 tonnes of ammunition was quickly ignited after several rockets managed to penetrate the main hold and, within ten minutes, the ship was at the bottom of the sea. The defending flak ship was also sunk and a Danish MV was left seriously damaged. As the main force wheeled away from the convoy another German MV was attacked by those who had any remaining ammunition. It was left burning but remained defiantly afloat as the force set course for home. During the initial assault three Mosquitos had been hit by flak and all decided to make for Sweden. Two landed safely but one 235 Squadron Mosquito, which had lost an engine due to the flak crashed at Getterøn.

Sorties from Banff were now restricted to ASR searches and, on May 21, both 143 and 248 Squadrons were still looking for U-boats who were not aware that the war was now over. On May 25, 143 and 404 Squadron were

disbanded, only for 14 Squadron to rise from the ashes of 143 Squadron the same day, still equipped with the Mosquito. The next day, 333 Squadron were disbanded into 334 Squadron which moved to Gardermoen on June 8, 1945 to become part of the Royal Norwegian Air Force. No 489 Squadron moved in from Dallachy to convert from the Beaufighter to the Mosquito FB.VI but this was to be short-lived as the squadron was disbanded on August 1, becoming the last Mosquito unit to operate from Banff. No 235 Squadron was also disbanded on July 10, and 248 Squadron temporarily escaped the axe when it was moved to Chivenor on July 19, 1945. ✤

Informal group photograph of 4 Squadron and their Mosquito FB.6s (as the FB.VI was known post-war), possibly at Celle. The squadron was re-formed at Volkel on September 1, 1945 and operated the Mosquito until July 1950 when the type was replaced by the Vampire FB.5. *Aeroplane*

The Aeroplane, June 29, 1945 By Flt Lt P Hansor Lester

Flying the DH Mosquito

THE FOLLOWING ARTICLE on the de Havilland Mosquito is by a pilot with experience of flying several Marks of the type. It is not expected nor intended to be of great interest to operational pilots who regularly fly this particular aeroplane and may have more experience of it than the author. The Aeroplane must, however, have many readers who have never flown Mosquitoes, who are never likely to fly them, or, perhaps, even, who don't want to fly them, who will welcome the opportunity of learning something about the handling qualities of one of the outstanding aeroplanes of this nation in both the West and East campaigns.

'As the aeroplane is crossing the hedge the throttles are cut, the speed drops off to about 125mph, and the aeroplane is eased on to the ground.' *Aeroplane*

FIRST IN THE FIELD – The prototype Mosquito W4050 takes off for a test flight during the original manufacturers' trials. This prototype bomber had two Rolls-Royce Merlin 21 engines and a span of 52ft 6ins: the short nacelles are also noticeable. *Aeroplane*

Settling in

THE FIRST thing that strikes one on looking at a Mosquito is its beauty of line, its clean, smooth taper, and many have remarked that this D.H. product recalls a thoroughbred racehorse.

For a normal-sized man to climb into a Mosquito while wearing a seat-type parachute is almost a physical impossibility (particularly in the case of the Marks III, VI, etc., which have the door in the side instead of in the floor), so the best entry is by climbing the ladder, hauling up the brolly and then putting in some hard work laying it out in the seat. The pilot can then descend the ladder again, take a quick look under the motor nacelles to check that the undercarriage locks have been removed, glance at the top of the fin to see that the pitot tube is uncovered, and do a manual check to see that the rear hatch is securely fastened, for should this hatch blow off in flight, serious things can happen to the empennage.

Once settled in and the harness done up, the pilot is impressed by the comfort of the seat, and the ease of accessibility of the ancillary controls - two points which some constructors might note as being of particular interest to pilots. The system of operating the petrol cocks is also too simple to be readily credited to all constructors of British operational aircraft. Just behind the pilot's seat

are two cocks marked 'Left' and 'Right,' and they can be turned so that they are both pointing inwards (towards each other) or both pointing outwards (away from each other); this signifies inwards for inner tanks and outwards for outer tanks. I am writing now of the ordinary production Mosquito which was not fitted with fuselage tank, drop tanks, rocket projectile rails, radar or any other operational excrescences, and the normal system of petrol-cock operation is, briefly, that you take-off and land on your outer tanks and fly at other times on your inner, or main tanks.

Engine start

The two Rolls-Royce Merlin motors have to be primed from the outside by the airman on the ground by hand, and have not the advantages of the U.S. practice of electric priming operated by the pilot from inside the cockpit; however, very seldom does a Merlin become temperamental and refuse to start, and so soon as the coolant temperature has reached 60° each motor may be run up, the magnetos tested, and the pitch controls exercised. Since there is a hydraulic pump on each motor, one motor should be throttled right back and the flaps lowered and raised with the other motor set at 2,000 rpm, and then the procedure reversed.

For taxiing, the aeroplane is responsive to the throttle, and with a bit of practice very little brake will be found necessary. However, when the brakes are used, either for taxying or at the end of the landing run, they should be used in short, sharp squeezes of the brake lever, as holding the brakes on is inclined to make the aeroplane swing about in a rather untidy manner.

On arrival at the take-off point a brief cockpit drill is carried out as follows. (I think that most people have their own method of checking the cockpit, but the following method is quite satisfactory). Set the elevator trimmer to

1¼° nose down and the rudder trim to neutral. Check that the oil temperatures and coolant temperatures are within the laid-down limits, and tighten the throttle friction nut. The mixture control is entirely automatic, so no check is necessary on this. The pitch controls are, of course, in the fully forward position, giving maximum rpm (approximately 8,000 at take-off boost, which is between plus 8¾ lb. and plus 12 lb., according to the mark of motor installed). Check that the petrol cocks are on the outer tanks, and that the fuel gauges are reading satisfactorily. The radiator shutters, which are worked by the brake-pressure system, are controlled by two small switches usually mounted next to the rudder trimmer, and are either fully open or fully closed (on certain marks they are manually operated by two hand cranks) and for take-off they should be set to fully open. The generator (which is driven by the starboard motor only) should be switched on and the gyros checked.After this the pilot need only clear each motor for a couple of seconds, lower about 15° of flap and he is ready to take-off.On a decent sized runway there is really no need to use flap for take-off but the Mosquito takes rather a long time initially to reach her single-motor safety speed after take-off, and in practice the use of a little flap has been found to lower this safety speed in proportion to the time taken to reach it.

Taxy for take-off

While taking-off the throttles should be opened rather more slowly than on most other aircraft, and in general practice to run up the motors and 'hold her on the brakes' is entirely unnecessary. As the throttles are opened a Mosquito tends to swing slightly to the left, which is checked by advancing the port throttle a little ahead of the starboard throttle. Until one is thoroughly used to the aeroplane (by which time it should not be necessary) take-off swing could be checked by

NIGHT SKY RAIDER — de Havilland Mosquito II night fighters achieved considerable success in thwarting the Luftwaffe attacks on London. This picture: A Mosquito II is seen in the matt black camouflage of 1942. *Aeroplane*

use of the brakes. If the throttles are opened at all 'ham-fistedly,' or too rapidly, the swing will develop quite viciously and tend to become almost uncontrollable, a fact which reacts most unfavourably upon the undercarriage, but if they are opened smoothly and slowly the swing is scarcely perceptible, even although the aeroplane is accelerating very rapidly. By the time the motors have been given approximately plus 1 lb. or 2 lb. boost, the tail should be well up and plenty of rudder control available and then the rest of the boost can be poured in. The throttle levers have a stop at take-off boost setting but by releasing two trip catches on the levers a pilot can go through the gate and obtain approximately another 6 lb. of boost, but the use of this is seldom found to be necessary in general practice.

The aircraft can safely be allowed to leave the ground at about 110-115mph, and a slight movement of the control column to the right is usually necessary to prevent a tendency to drop the left wing. The undercarriage comes up at quite a normal rate, and when the lights have gone out (there is, by the way, no visual indicator for the position of the retractable tail-wheel) the pilot can throttle back to plus 6 lb. boost and 2,650 rpm and climb to the desired height. The indicated airspeed during the initial part of the climb should be 150mph until the flaps are raised, when it will very rapidly increase to 180mph, which is 10mph above the safety speed for single-motor flying without use of flap. The actual raising of the flaps produces a very strong nose-down effect, but very slight backward movement of the elevator trimmer will correct this, as the trimmer itself is very sensitive.

When the coolant temperatures have dropped below 95° (once again certain marks of motors run at higher temperatures than this) the radiator shutters may be closed, and this action - initially much to the pilot's surprise - also produces strong nose-down effect. These little shutters are set underneath the radiator, which is built into the leading edge of the wing and are similar in appearance to the very small s.t.e. flaps which have been mounted half-way along the wind chord, and they are extraordinarily strong; so much so, that if you trim the aeroplane to fly straight and level with 'hands off,' and shutters open, then smartly close the shutters, the resultant nose-down effect is so strong that the motors will cut under the effect of negative G, and the aeroplane will go into a steep dive. However, in normal usage the form is to close the shutters with the right hand and re-trim the aeroplane at the same time with the left hand.

Having climbed to the desired height the pilot throttles back to plus 4 lb. boost and 2,400 rpm, and changes the petrol cocks over on to main tanks. Naturally if he is going to climb up pretty high, he should have changed them earlier, but for the sake of argument he is just going to have a little ride around at about 3,000ft. At the present revs and boost, which is the optimum for indefinite cruising, the aircraft settles down to an easy cruising speed of approximately 270mph, and the time has come to start turning gently round the sky in order to feel the controls. The Mosquito is very positive in the pitching plane and extremely sensitive to

PUGNACITY — The well-armed Mosquito VI carries, in this photograph, eight rocket-firing projectiles and four .303 machine-guns and four 20mm cannons. *Aeroplane*

uncomfortably high attitude and the aeroplane feels quite reluctant to stall at all! However, a little perseverance coaxes her into the stall and the nose whips down quite viciously with a tendency to drop the right wing. There is naturally a pretty violent change in the attitude of the aeroplane now, but by applying the normal corrective methods of stick forward, throttles open and picking up the wing with firm (but not necessarily full) opposite rudder, normal flight is regained with remarkably little loss of height. Naturally when the recovery from the stall is effected with flaps lowered care must be taken to see that the air speed does not exceed the maximum allowable for use of flap, which is 150mph, in the ensuing dive.

Single engine handling

So far we have seen that the Mosquito is easy to take off, extremely light and pleasant to handle in normal flight, and, unless treated in a thoroughly unladylike manner, is not unkind in stalled conditions. Let us now see how she will react in the event of one of her 'fans' going off duty.

We will assume the pilot is flying

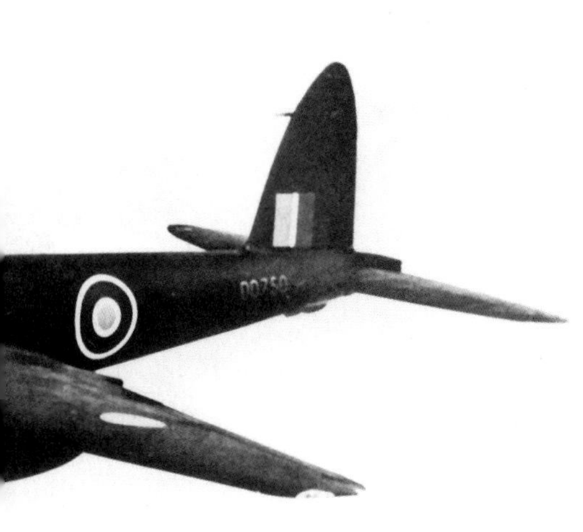

DOUBLE FACED — The Mosquito VI could be used as a fighter-bomber; this 4 Squadron machine displays a pair of 500lb bombs but was also armed with machine-guns as well. *Aeroplane*

the trimmer; thus in actual cross-country flying, to trim it to fly hands off and maintain a constant height is not easy; however, only a light touch of the hand resting on the control column is necessary to remedy this. In the rolling plane she is almost unbelievably light on the ailerons and in the yawing plane she does not react favourably to coarse use of the rudder; gentle and medium turns can be very satisfactorily effected with the feet resting on the floor instead of on the rudder pedals without the top needle of the turn and bank indicator registering any protest.

Stalling

To stall a Mosquito both throttles must be pulled back and the nose raised. With the throttles fully closed and the horn blaring (there is no switch to eliminate this, so it has to be endured as a gentle reminder) the pilot allows air speed to drop off and cannot help observing that she loses speed very slowly in comparison to some of the less streamlined flying Christmas trees, and he also notices that there is little tendency to mush and lose

height as he approaches the stalling point. Observation of the actual speed at which the aeroplane stalls is not easy as the needle of the A.S.I. flickers very violently, but plenty of warning is given before the stall because at about 125mph the aeroplane starts vibrating and juddering in no uncertain manner. At about 115mph she stalls completely, but not in any way viciously, and with flaps and wheels up, the nose drops quite sharply but without any tendency to drop a wing with flaps and wheels down and the motors throttled right back there is little difference in behaviour except that the speeds of the preliminary warning and the stall itself are about 15 miles an hour less, the nose has to be held a little higher, and she loses a little more height before actually stalling. To stall with flaps and wheels down and about minus one boost and 2,400 revs on each motor is not quite such a care-free manoeuvre, but to see how she behaves in this condition is interesting, and does not really present any difficulty. The air speed gets down somewhere in the region of 85 to 90mph and the nose has to be held in an

peacefully around the sky at 3,000ft at 270mph with plus four boost and 2,400 revs on each motor and, since the generator is driven by the starboard motor, the port airscrew is feathered. This is very rapidly done by pressing the port feathering button on the dashboard and holding it in for a second just to make sure that the solenoid has engaged. Immediately the revs start to decrease, and as they do so the pilot fully closes the port throttle and in a very few seconds the port airscrew is fully feathered and stationary beside. The aeroplane's reaction to this is a fairly sharp swing to port, but, owing to the servo rudder control, this is very easily corrected with a gentle but firm pressure of the right foot on the rudder pedal. A fair amount of rudder trim (about two or three turns) relieves this, and, having opened the starboard radiator shutter, slight application of tail-heavy trim on the elevator, enables the aero-plane to be flown 'hands off' with no trouble. With normal load at this height there is no necessity to open up the starboard motor from its present setting in order to maintain

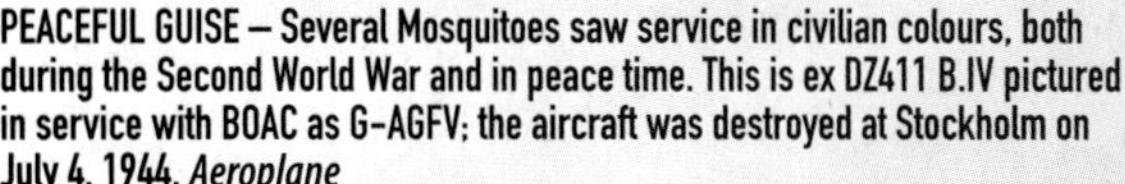

PEACEFUL GUISE — Several Mosquitoes saw service in civilian colours, both during the Second World War and in peace time. This is ex DZ411 B.IV pictured in service with BOAC as G–AGFV; the aircraft was destroyed at Stockholm on July 4, 1944. *Aeroplane*

height at approximately 180mph, but at 2,650 revs and plus six boost an easy cruising speed of 200 to 210mph can be maintained. The aeroplane can also be trimmed to execute with 'hands off' perfect rate two turns without loss of height or airspeed in either direction! This is indeed 'a little something which the others haven't got.' And when the controls are taken in hand again, and the starboard motor opened up a little further, quite tight, steep turns in either direction can be done. I have even watched Geoffrey de Havilland, junior, carry out upward rolls with one motor feathered, although I must confess I have not aspired to try it myself.

While on the subject of aerobatics I do not propose to go into the details of how to perform each individual manoeuvre, but will only say that normal aerobatics present no difficulty whatsoever, manoeuvres in the rolling plane being particularly easy to execute. Nor do I intend to go into the operational aspect of the aeroplane or discuss its maximum speed under various conditions or its climb and performance figures at various altitudes. Almost all normal aerobatics can be carried out with no trouble at all (but the 'Mossie' is not a good aeroplane in which to practise either right or left-hand spins!) but if you want to push the nose down and throw her about a bit, you will not find her short of knots.

Approach

However, to return to more peaceful pursuits; we will now assume the pilot unfeathers the port 'fan' and see how he gets on with a normal approach and landing. Before we leave the subject of the Mosquito's amazing single-motor performance I would like to add that the single-motor approach and landing is easier to do well, either with or without the airscrew feathered, than on any other type of twin motor aircraft which I have flown, and I have on more than one occasion started an overshoot procedure at 500ft and gone round again with flaps and wheels down without any difficulty whatsoever, provided always that a safety speed of at least 145mph has been maintained on the approach. I must also admit that I have seen people endeavour to go round again after their speed had dropped below this figure, and on all occasions they came to grief.

To unfeather the airscrew the pilot first of all checks that the port ignition switches are on and that the port pitch control is in the fully coarse position. He then opens the port throttle to the normal starting-up position (about ¾in. open), pushes in the port feathering button and holds in it. If he looks at the port airscrew he can see the blades gradually twisting to assume some positive pitch and in a second or two the airscrew starts to revolve. Almost immediately the motor fires and the revs start to build up on the revolution indicator, and when they have reached 1,000 rpm he releases the feathering button and slips one finger into the little hole behind it to make sure that it has returned to the normal position. This is rather important, because just occasionally the solenoid sticks and the button does not come out with the result that the revs are pushed up by the unfeathering mechanism until they are beyond the control of the constant-speed unit, and once the airscrew starts to windmill freely the revs build up to about 3,750 rpm, and the poor old Merlin starts to make a noise like a mass formation of Harvards taking-off, a state of affairs which is not recommended in the Rolls-Royce Merlin handling notes. (The cure for this eventuality is to pull the button out by hand and raise the nose fairly steeply; this produces a drop in airspeed, and since the airscrew is not governed by a c.s.u. the revs drop back until they eventually come within the range of the pitch control and are once more governed by its manual setting in the cockpit.)

Now the motor is turning over at 1,000 rpm (although in practice they may have built up a little higher), and if the coolant temperature is such that to warm up at low revs is not necessary the pilot can move the constant-speed lever forward until both motors are showing the same rpm; he then moves the throttle forward until the boost readings for both motors are the same, at the same time neutralizing the rudder trimmer. If he now closes the starboard radiator shutter he returns to our previous happy state of cruising at something over 250mph.

On arriving back at the aerodrome and having selected the runway, the pilot descends to about 1,500ft and throttles back as far as he can without being inflicted with the horn blowing. He is then endeavouring to lose enough speed to permit him to operate the landing gear, and at this stage of our flight the excellency of the Mosquito's streamline is most apparent. To lose the hundred odd miles per hour which is the

'I think that the Mosquito is one of the easiest aircraft there is in which to make a good landing whether it be a tail-high 'wheeler' or in a three-point attitude.' This Australian-built T.43 is just about to touchdown for a 'near' three-pointer. *Via Martyn Chorlton*

'In the rolling plane she is almost unbelievably light on the ailerons and in the yawing plane she does not react favourably to coarse use of the rudder.............' *Aeroplane*

difference between cruising speed and the maximum permissible speed for lowering the wheels and at the same time maintain a constant height, takes much longer than one would expect. On the other hand, when the pilot has lowered the wheels at 180mph, he has to put on as much as plus 2 lb. or 3 lb. boost in order to maintain 160mph without losing height. This is because the somewhat massive undercarriage destroys the smoothness of the Mosquito's form and she becomes quite a different aeroplane to handle, losing much of her sensitivity.

Landing

At this stage of events the petrol cocks are turned over to outer tanks, the radiator shutters opened, and the aeroplane trimmed to continue flying at 160mph. As the pilot turns across wind, he lowers the flaps; these can be let down all at once, and have a very powerful nose-up effect. This is naturally countered by easing the nose down and winding the elevator trimmer well forward, trimming the aeroplane to fly at 140mph with flaps fully down, and adjusting the boost setting to give the desired rate of descent to the rapidly approaching runway beneath. As he turns into wind the airspeed must not be allowed to drop below 140mph, as in the event of a motor failure he wants to be able to have at least 145mph available in order to maintain perfect control. Thus he maintains this seemingly high approach speed right down until coming over the hedge. At about 600ft the pilot eases the pitch controls to the fully fine position and settles down to the final approach. As the aeroplane is crossing the hedge the throttles are cut, the speed drops off to about 125mph, and the aeroplane is eased on to the ground. I think that the Mosquito is one of the easiest aircraft there is in which to make a good landing whether it be a tail-high 'wheeler' or in a three-point attitude. As the aeroplane is checked close to the ground she loses speed rapidly, and by moving the control column back a little to prevent her sinking too rapidly, she just cushions on to the ground. Without using much brake, the 'Mossie' has a very short landing run in relation to such a high approach speed, and with a 10 to 15mph wind nobody should have any difficulty in landing in 600yds; it has been done many time in a 450yd field.

If a really smooth landing has been made and there is no appreciable cross-wind the 'Mossie' has no tendency to swing at all, and will just quietly roll to a stop, but if the wind is a little on the port side, or if the arrival is not quite in the highest traditions of the Central Flying School, she may tend to swing slightly to port. This is easily corrected by a short, sharp squeeze of the brake lever. (May I remind you here that prolonged holding of the brakes nearly always result in over-correction? Two or three short 'puffs' will cure any swing which may occur under normal circumstances.)

All that is left now is for the pilot to raise the flaps, taxi back, disperse her, turn all the taps off, and the flight is over. My own opinion is that there is no aeroplane more delightful to fly in than the Mosquito, and should readers who have more recent practice on them than I disagree with my procedure, I can only reiterate that this article is intended purely as of objective interest to those who have not driven one. ✤

The prototype Mosquito W4050 in one of its many schemes, in this case with the original all yellow scheme 'toned down' (from above at least) by the application of standard RAF camouflage upper surfaces. *Andy Hay/www.flyingart.co.uk*

XD-N
TK620 XD

Mosquito B.35s VP185, VP194 and TK620 line up on RAF Hemswell's runway 06 not long after the unit made the short move from Coningsby in April 1950. *Aeroplane*

Secondary duties

One of the most prolific roles for the Mosquito was as a trainer, and the trainer variant was made available to the RAF from as early as September 1942. 'Mossie' Trainers continued to serve long after the end of World War Two, as did the 'Target Tug' variants, and these would become the last of the breed in service.

T.III TV959 seen prior to delivery to 13 OTU at Middle St George in August 1945. She went on to serve with 54 OTU, 228 OCU, 204 AFS (Advanced Flying School), HCEU (Home Command Examining Unit), FCCS (Fighter Command Communication Squadron) and 1 CAACU. The aircraft was presented to the Imperial War Museum in 1963 and later sold to Paul Allen's Flying Heritage Collection at Paine Field in Everett, Washington. She became the second Mosquito that AVspecs Ltd. restored to flying condition at Auckland, New Zealand. *Aeroplane*

T.III VT589 in all-yellow training scheme during its service with 58 Squadron. The Mosquito transferred to 540 Squadron but, on April 24, 1951, swung on landing at Benson, causing the undercarriage to collapse; the aircraft was not repaired. *Andy Hay/www.flyingart.co.uk*

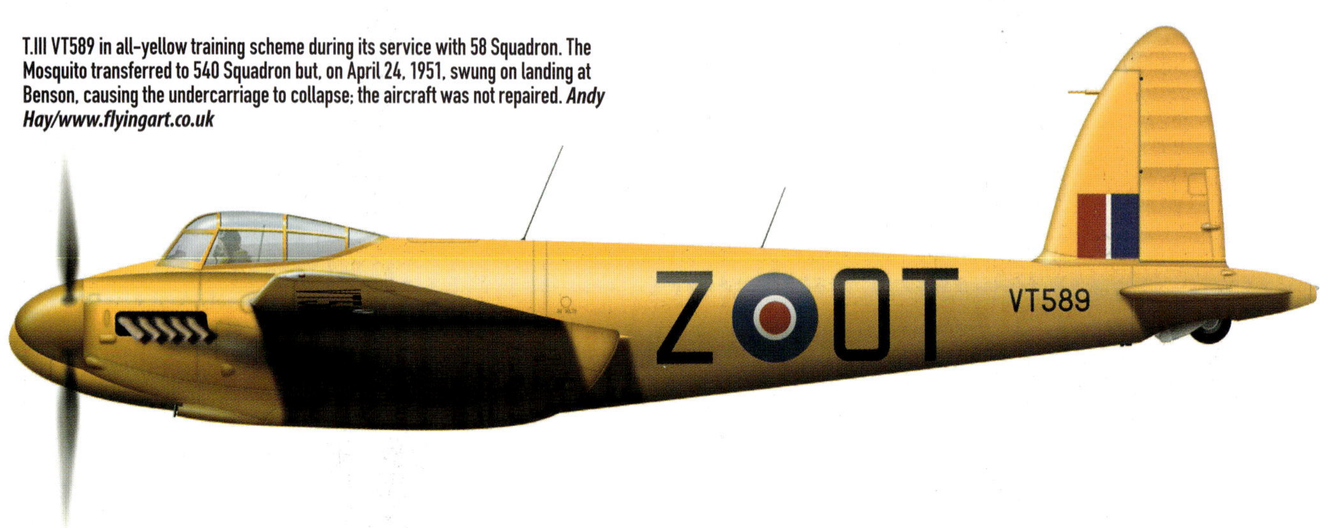

The very first of the 362 Mosquito T.IIIs built was W4053, pictured here at Boscombe Down in September 1942. The aircraft spent its flying career with de Havilland and later with 16 OTU at Upper Heyford until that unit disbanded in 1947. *Aeroplane*

The Trainers

The T.III - From the outset, the two-seat design of the Mosquito made it most suitable for conversion to a trainer, unlike many other military aircraft designed during World War Two that launched a trainee pilot into the 'wild blue' without the comfort of an instructor alongside.

The Mosquito T.III was fitted with dual controls but without armament and were powered by Merlin 21, 23 or 25 engines. Fully loaded, complete with a pair of 100 gal drop tanks, the T.III weighed in at 20,319lb. The prototype was W4053 which first flew in the hands of Geoffrey de Havilland from Hatfield on January 30, 1942.

The first unit to receive the T.III was the MCU (Mosquito Conversion Unit), later redesignated as 1655 MTU (Mosquito Training Unit). It was formed at Horsham St Faith in August 1942 but had moved to Marham by the end of the following month. By October, several were already arriving on operational units, including night fighter squadrons who used them to convert Beaufighter crews to the Mosquito without them leaving the unit. OTUs (Operational Training Units) were the next in line to receive the T.III in bulk; 60 OTU, which had reformed at High Ercall, was first and, later in the war, 8, 13, 16, 51 and 54 OTU also received the type.

Post war, the type was still prevalent with Flying Training Command and formed the backbone of 204 AFS which was established at Cottesmore on March 15, 1947 until it was moved to Bassingbourn to become 'D' Flight of 231 OCU (Operational Conversion Unit) in February 1952.

Three hundred and sixty two Mosquito T.IIIs were built, all but 78 of them at Leavesden, the remainder at Hatfield. The type served with a host of squadrons, training units, wings, and station flights (see Chapter 21) until it was retired in 1963.

T.III production - A/c W4053 (Prototype), HJ851-HJ899, HJ958-HJ999, LR516-LR541, LR553-LR585, RR270-RR319, TV954-TV984, TW101-TW119, VA871-VA894, VA923-VA928, VP342-VP355, VR330-VR349, VT581-VT596 and VT604-VT631.

Built as a B.35, RS719 only served with the ETPS (Empire Test Pilot School) before being converted as the prototype TT.35. The aircraft went on to serve the TRE (Telecommunications Research Establishment), A&AEE, 3 CAACU, the THUM (Temperature & Humidity) Flight at Woodvale and finally 5 CAACU before being SOC on May 31, 1958. *Aeroplane* ▼

Canada and Australian trainers

The T.III was not the only trainer version of the Mosquito. In Canada, the T.22 was produced, based on the FB.21. The dual controlled aircraft was powered by a pair of Packard-Merlin 33 engines. Only six T.22s were built: KA873 to KA876 and KA896 and KA897. De Havilland Canada also built the T.27 which was a development of the T.22 powered by Packard-Merlin 225 engines. Nineteen of these were built: KA877 to KA895.

In Australia, a trainer was developed from the FB.40 and designated the T.43. The Mosquito only differed from the fighter bomber by having dual controls and dual elevator trim tabs. Twenty two T.43s were built.

The Tugs

TT.35 - Modified from the B.35, 27 Mosquitoes, the vast majority from storage, were converted into target tugs by Brooklands Aviation Ltd and at Sywell and re-designated as the TT.35. The main modification was the fitment of a ML Type G wind-driven target winch under the fuselage. TT.35s mainly served with the CAACUs (Civilian Anti-Aircraft Co-Operation Units) as well as several OCUs and TTFs (Target Towing Flights). The RAF's TT.35s were the final Mosquito variants to serve, the last retiring in 1963.

TT.6 - Two FB.VIs were selected for conversion to target tugs for the Belgian Air Force. The conversion work was carried out at Ringway by the Fairey Aviation Company during late 1953 and early 1954. The two aircraft, ex TE663 and ex TE771, were delivered to the Belgian Air Force as MC-2 and MC-3 respectively and served until late 1956.

TT.39 - (See Chapter 16) ❖

Mosquito T.IIIs TV959 and RR299 pictured before they were delivered to 13 and 51 OTUs respectively. Both aircraft had very busy military careers. RR299/G-ASKH was owned and operated by British Aerospace and was lost at the Barton airshow on July 21, 1996, when she was the last airworthy de Havilland DH.98 Mosquito. TV959 was placed in the care of the Imperial War Museum but was then sold to Paul Allen's Flying Heritage Collection who had it restored to airworthy condition by Avspecs, Ardmore, New Zealand.
Aeroplane

All at sea

The Royal Navy flew twelve different variants of the Mosquito between 1944 and 1953 but only three of these were prefixed with the word 'Sea'. David H. Smith takes a closer look at the dedicated Sea Mosquito 33, 37 and 39.

Lt Cdr Eric 'Winkle' Brown lands Mosquito FB.VI, LR359 on HMS *Indefatigable* on March 25, 1944. This was the first landing on an aircraft carrier by a Mosquito, and the first twin-engined deck landing since Jimmy Doolittle's B-25 Mitchells in April 1942 for their famous raid on Tokyo. *Via Martyn Chorlton*

Proving the theory

The Royal Navy had been operating various marks of Mosquito from not long after its introduction into RAF service. However, at this stage the aircraft was firmly land based but plans were evolving which would allow the Mosquito to be operated from a carrier in a front-line, operational capacity.

Despite the success of the Mosquito aircraft carrier trials that followed, the Mosquito was never adopted for operations at sea but this did not stop three dedicated Sea Mosquito marks being produced.

The Sea Mosquito TF/TR.33

Based on the Mosquito FB.VI, the Sea Mosquito TF (Torpedo/Fighter) later TR (Torpedo/Reconnaissance) Mk 33 was the first fully dedicated Royal Navy variant designed for carrier operations. The TR.33 was described in detail in The Aeroplane in 1946; the following is an excerpt:-

Since the first delivery of Mosquitoes to the RAF in July, 1941, these aircraft have enjoyed unrivalled popularity in almost every Command and theatre night or day during the later stages of hostilities in Europe it would have been reasonably safe to wager that at least one Mosquito would be in the air. Quite recently a new version of Mosquito was introduced for Naval carrier-borne work, with four cannons, an 18in torpedo or alternative loads of bombs and RPs. The TR.33, or Sea Mosquito, has manually folding wings and arrester hook, also a modified nose to take a American ASH nose radar equipment. Basically, it is a development of the FB.VI. Considerable modification to wing structure has naturally been entailed, as the Mosquito wing was never intended to fold. In a manner rather similar to that employed on the Sea Hornet, Alclad sheet has been let into the top and bottom wing surfaces both inboard and outboard of the folding joint. The span-wise stringers in the skin have been cut down slightly and are sandwiched between the alloy sheets. The two ribs at the folding point are made up of thick Alclad-spruce-Alclad sandwich webs with laminated booms. The alloy sheet is 18 gauge and, with the spruce, the web of the rib is 1¾in thick. Redux bonding is used at the metal-to-wood joints.

The outer wing section folds on four centrally-disposed tight alloy hinges, and the latch pins and their pick-up fittings are bolted to the lower booms of the two main spars. The bolts have a mechanical lock and are withdrawn simultaneously when a large spring-loaded lever is folded down and rearwards from the wing joint. Positive locking is confirmed by the retraction of two red flags on the upper wing surface at the folding point. The aileron controls are carried past the folding point in short sections of heavy Bowden cable, and small spring-loaded doors in the skin are closed by levers operated by buffers as the wings reach the fully spread position.

The wings are folded by a crew of three

Sea Mosquito TR.33s of 771 Squadron at Lee-on-Solent, a unit that flew the type from May 1947 to March 1950. *Aeroplane*

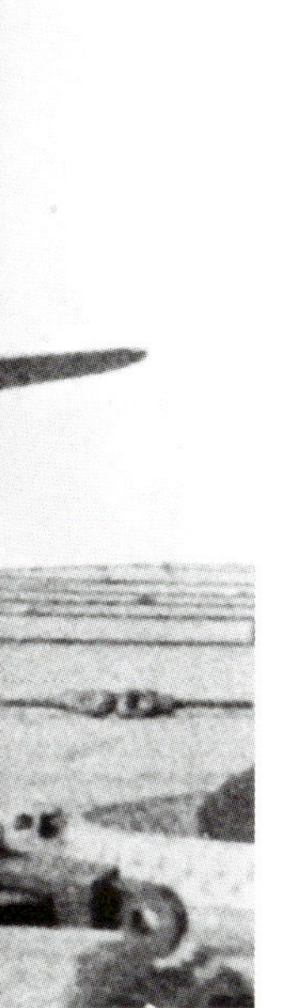

or four using a pole and the hinge point is immediately outboard of the flaps. Flap and aileron shrouds have been modified, but all other exterior wing features are unchanged. In the folded position, the wing tips are held down by elastic ropes to lugs on the rear hoop of the cockpit enclosure, and the weight is supported by jury struts to the inboard wing sections. The jury struts are inserted from inside the undercarriage wheel-well through a spring flap in the top wing surface, and at the lower end.

Trimming Tab Lock

When the wing is folded on existing Sea Mosquitoes, the aileron trimming tab on the port wing is disconnected by the separation of two small gear wheels, and catches are automatically engaged with the teeth of the gears to prevent movement and consequent maladjustment, until re-engagement takes place.

Among modifications to the structure of the Sea Mosquito is the introduction of a bulkhead in the fuselage above the attachment points of the arrester hook, and the inclusion of two "straights" similar to those used on the Sea Hornet. The straights are large laminated longerons stretching from the arrester hook attachment points to the rear wing spar. The hook is bolted through the fuselage wall to the straights, and they are in turn bolted, via modified fittings, to the rear main wing spar at its attachment points. The fuselage is otherwise standard, but some reinforcement will be included in the next aircraft, so that RATOG (Rocket Assisted Take-Off Gear) may be employed. The weight sacrifice for folding wings, used for the first time on a highly-stressed monoplane wing of wood construction, is just over 300 lb.

Later Sea Mosquitoes have smaller wheels (those used on the Beaufighter) and Lockheed

The Sea Mosquito TR.33 loaded and folded. This photograph of the prototype shows the four-bladed airscrews, the slinging of the 18in torpedo, and, on the folded wings, the 50 gallon drop tanks for which bombs may be substituted. The standard D.H. undercarriage is replaced by Lockheed hydraulic legs on the production aircraft. *Aeroplane*

hydraulic shock-absorber legs, but trials with the prototype were carried out with the standard undercarriage.

The torpedo is slung externally, and is supported by a tubular fitting bolted at the top end to the front main wing spar at the point of the c.g. Two drag struts are led to number four bulkhead below the pilot, and the rear steady points are braced from the rear cannon-support members. When the torpedo is carried, the bomb doors are closed and the bomb bay empty; the alternative load is two 500lb bombs stowed internally, and either two more 500lb bombs under the wings, or RPs.

To assist in take-off, the Sea Mosquito has

TR.33 TW256 originally served with 703 Squadron and was then transferred to 771 Squadron as depicted. Finally the aircraft was operated by Airwork until an engine failed on take-off and the undercarriage collapsed at Hurn in April 1953.
Andy Hay/www.flyingart.co.uk

a large diameter (12ft 6in) four-bladed airscrews which give a thrust improvement of 5-10%. The engines are Rolls-Royce Merlin 25s with a take-off rating of 1,620hp at 3,000rpm and + 18lb boost. This figure is nearly 100hp more than recent marks of Mosquito.

Deck-landing Trials

All carrier-borne squadrons are at present equipped with single-engine aircraft, and until the spring of 1944 no attempt had been made to operate a twin from the deck of an aircraft carrier. However, at that time it became apparent that Naval operations might be handicapped in the future by the restrictions in size, range, accommodation, etc., imposed by the exclusive use of single-engine aircraft. It was decided, therefore, that deck-landing trials with twin-engine aircraft should be instituted without delay, and a Mosquito FB.VI was selected as being representative of modern high-performance twins.

The trials were carried out on March 25 and 26, 1944, from HMS *Indefatigable* and Mosquito LR359 was piloted by Lt Cdr E M Brown, MBE, DSC. One of the Navy's most experienced 'batsmen' joined the ship for the trials, and his job called for particular skill and agility as the engine nacelles made it difficult for the pilot to see him on the approach unless he stood dead ahead of the aircraft until touch-down. The pilot's view on the approach for deck landing is very good in all other respects and no complaints were made.

The Mosquito took off and landed successfully seven times during the first trials, but on the eighth landing the arrester hook was fractured. The pilot opened-up immediately and, fortunately, was able to take off again.

On the second series of deck landings, made on May 9 and 10, Lt Cdr Brown and Cdr H J F Lane took off and landed seventeen times without mishap, although on one occasion the arrester hook failed to pick up the wire and the pilot had to depend upon his wheel brakes to bring the aircraft to a standstill.

Following these successful trials with the FB.VI, production was started of a Naval Mosquito with folding wings, deck-arrester gear, a modified nose to carry radar equipment, and provision for a torpedo or a 2,000lb bomb.

Sea Mosquito Performance

The performance of the TR.33 is an all-round compromise in view of its diverse duties. It is important to mention that no attempt has been made to operate this mark at maximum conditions comparable with those expected in wartime. With assisted take-off, the present maximum weight of approximately 22,000lb (49lb/sq ft wing loading) could certainly be increased. It will be remembered that the Mk 16, with less power and without assistance, but on a full-length runway, took off at weights up to 25,200lb with a wing loading of 56lb/sq ft. The width of the TR.33 with wings folded, is 27ft 3in, and the height 13ft 6in.

One reason for limiting the peacetime weight figures for the aircraft is to make sure that single-engine flying shall be possible without undue risk and with power in hand. Normally, Mosquito single-engine performance has always been extremely good,

A Sea Mosquito TR.33 on approach to HMS *Indefatigable* during further carrier trials in 1946. *RAE via Aeroplane*

Ex-B.XVI PF606 following conversion to a TT.39 by General Aircraft Ltd. The aircraft survived until it was SOC at Lossiemouth on November 27, 1952. *Andy Hay/www.flyingart.co.uk*

but with three paddle blades, or with four blades, the wind-milling drag of an airscrew is high and, should an engine refuse to feather, an appropriate increase in power and single-engine safety speed is called for. In addition, for reasons of economy in fuel, and reduction of wear and tear on components, it is to be expected that the use of maximum power out-put will be discouraged for all normal flying.

Sea Mosquito TR.33 in service

The TR.33 served with nine FAA (Fleet Air Arm) units between April 1946 and October 1950, all but one of them in a front-line capacity. Only 811 Squadron, which had reformed at Ford on September 15, 1945 with Mosquito FB.VIs, would receive the TR.33 from April 1946. A dozen were taken on strength but, by the time the squadron moved to Brawdy in December 1946, half of them had already been withdrawn. Following another move to Eglinton in March 1947, the TR.33's brief operational career came to an end when 811 Squadron was disbanded on July 1, 1947.

One interesting task carried out by a pair of TR.33s, TW228 and TW230 was their part in the secretive Highball trials. These two aircraft were the only Sea Mosquitoes allocated to an RAF unit, namely the Highball Trials Flight at Coningsby in Lincolnshire. The Highball bouncing bomb, designed by Barnes Wallis, had been in development since late 1942, with much of work being carried out by the Mosquito-equipped 618 Squadron. The officially named flight, however, only existed from January 1946 to November 1947.

The last TR.33s served the FAA until June 1953 with 751 Squadron at Watton in Norfolk. 53 were built in the serial ranges LR359, LR387, TS444, TS449, TW227-TW257 and NS586-NS589.

Sea Mosquito TF/TR.37

The TR.37 was virtually identical to the TR.33, with the exception of the radar, which gave the aircraft a 'bull' type nose. The reason for this was that the American radar was replaced by the British ASV Mk 13B. Only fourteen TR.37s were built in the serial range VT724-VT727. The type only served with 703 and 771 Squadrons between December 1948 and May 1950.

Sea Mosquito TT.39

A derivative of the B.XVI, the target-towing TT.39 was converted by General Aircraft Ltd. Work included extending the forward fuselage into a glazed nose for a camera operator and the fitment of a dorsal glazed observation cupola. Some of the 35 aircraft were converted with re-fitted with Merlin 72/73 engines and the nose modification extended the fuselage to a length of 43ft 4in. While the RAF continued to fly its dedicated TT.35s until 1956, only three squadrons of the FAA operated the TT.39 until May 1952. The final unit, 728 Squadron, retired the type at Hal Far, Malta. ❖

Sea Mosquito TF/TR.37

703 (VT728 '048/LP')	**Dec 1948 to May 1950**
	Lee-on-Solent, Ford
771 (TW240)	**Dec 1948 to Jul 1949**
	Ford, Evanton, Lee-on-Solent
RAE	

Sea Mosquito TT.39

703 (PF576)	**Oct 1948**
	Lee-on-Solent
728 (RV295 '511/HF')	**Mar 1949 to May 1952**
	Hal Far
771 (PF452 '598/FD')	**Jan 1950 to Jan 1952**
	Ford, Evanton, Lee-on-Solent
AAEE	

Sea Mosquito TF/TR.33 FAA Units

703 (TW233 'U')	**Jun 1946 to Oct 1950**
	Thorney Island, Lee-on-Solent, Ford
739 (TW294)	**May 1947 to Jul 1950**
	Culham
751 (TW250)	**Mar 1952 to Jun 1953**
	Watton
762 (TW283 '466/CW')	**Nov 1947 to Nov 1949**
	Ford, Culdrose
771 (TW277 '597/LP')	**May 1947 to Mar 1950**
	Ford, Evanton, Lee-on-Solent
778 (RF904 '042/FD')	**Apr 1946 to 1948**
	Ford, Tangmere, Lee-on-Solent
787 (TW234)	**Mar 1946 to Dec 1946**
	West Raynham
790 (TW281 '407/CW')	**Dec 1946 to Nov 1949**
	Dale, Culdrose
811 (TW268 'FD4G')	**Apr 1946 to Jul 1947**
	Ford, Brawdy, Eglinton

AAEE, Airwork, ARS Ford, ECFS, FRU, RAE, TRE, TREFU

The prototype TR.37, VT724, pictured in March 1948 during trials with the A&AEE at Boscombe Down. The Sea Mosquito served with 703 Squadron at Lee-on-Solent and Ford and finally the RAE. *Via Martyn Chorlton*

In 1948, an SM-1 (Mamba) engine was test flown under
a Mosquito, making it the first turbofan engine to fly.
The SM-1 engine was intended for the Swiss-built
EFW N-20 'Aiguillon' (Stinger)
jet fighter bomber.
Aeroplane

ARROW BOOKS
633
Squadron
FREDERICK
E. SMITH
2'- NET
COMPLETE AND
UNABRIDGED

Mosquito B.35, RS712, appeared in the film *633 Squadron* displaying the serial RF580 and the fictitious squadron codes, HT–F. RF580 was, in fact, originally a Mosquito FB.VI which was destroyed during a ferry flight in Iraq in 1945. *Via Martyn Chorlton*

633 Squadron

A classic British film featuring a classic British aircraft; François Prins looks at the 1964 film, 633 Squadron.

From novel to film

Frederick Smith wrote a novel about a crack RAF Mosquito squadron in the early 1960s. Entitled *633 Squadron,* it was a gripping story and spawned two further books dealing with the unit. Naturally, such a yarn attracted the film industry and a deal was struck and the screen rights to the first book were bought by the US Mirisch Company.

Smith's *633 Squadron* novel tells the story of the special Mosquito squadron chosen to attack a heavy-water plant in Norway; as a sub-plot it also deals with the Norwegian resistance and their exploits. From this one can see that there is some historic basis for the various episodes that are loosely based on Mosquito squadrons stationed in Scotland during the Second World War. The unit that is featured in the book and the film is located 'somewhere in England' and attacks targets in Norway. A lone Mosquito also bombs a Gestapo HQ where a leading member of the Norwegian resistance is being held.

Trawling for Mosquitoes

In 1962, the film company appointed recently-retired Group Captain T. G. 'Hamish' Mahaddie as aviation consultant and co-ordinator for *633 Squadron*. Mahaddie, a much-decorated former Pathfinder pilot, knew the Mosquito well and was already experienced in obtaining aircraft for film work and on how film companies function. In 1954, he had organised and overseen the Lancaster aircraft that were drawn from RAF stores for use in *The Dam Busters* film. Talking with Hamish some years later, he recalled the obtaining of Mosquitos for the film. *"We were very fortunate that 633 Squadron was made when it was, as there were still Mosquitos operating in the UK. Had it been left for a year or two I think we would have struggled. However, I*

Airspeed–built Mosquito B.35, RS709, pictured just after the filming of *633 Squadron*. The Mosquito displayed the serial HR113 (originally an FB.VI which became an instructional airframe in 1948) and, as well as the codes HT–D, as displayed, the aircraft appeared as HT–G as well. *Via Martyn Chorlton*

found that there were 16 examples in various states of repair. Seven were airworthy, or nearly so, one was in dismantled state, one crated for the Smithsonian Institute and the remainder in taxiable condition or in various pieces in store. The flying aircraft had recently been retired from 3 CACCU (Civilian Anti-Aircraft Co-operation Unit) at Exeter and were offered for sale. Before we could bid for the lot, one aircraft was sold to Hawker Siddeley and another to the Liverpool Corporation. Anyway we finished our survey and

bought nine aircraft, four airworthy and five to be roaded to the location, these we could use for airfield set dressing and possible taxi shots, that sort of thing. The airworthy aircraft were flown to RAF Bovingdon, which had been selected for filming, and the others arrived on trailers. I paid £75 each, fully fuelled, for the flying aircraft and between £45 and £35 for the others. The prices included delivery and a load of spares that the Exeter people and the RAF were glad to get rid of."

While Hamish dealt with the logistics on the ground, Captain John Crewdson of the Film Aviation Services Company was in overall charge of the airworthy aircraft. Crewdson was an experienced pilot who had supplied aircraft for various films, including the replica German aircraft, based on Tiger Moth airframes, for *Lawrence of Arabia*. One of Crewdson's pilots on *633 Squadron* was the late John 'Jeff' Hawke, who was then a flight lieutenant in the RAF and was later to become one of the

TT.35 RS718, which was used to represent the crash landing HJ898 during filming and was subsequently written off in the process. *Andy Hay/www.flyingart.co.uk*

leading suppliers of flying services to the film industry. Two other RAF officers joined Hawke, they were Flt Lt D J Curtis (RAF Locking) and Fg Off C Kirkham DFC (RAF Little Rissington). Peter Warden and Taff Rich, who had worked with Crewdson previously, also joined the flying team. For pilot training on type, the dual control Mosquito T.III (TW117) was used and Crewdson found that, on average, pilots required 90 minutes on the T.III before converting to the TT.35s.

The airworthy Mosquitos were: RS709, RS712, TA639, TA719 and TW117, of which RS709 and RS712 were Airspeed-built B.35s converted to TT.35s. TA639 and TA719 were De Havilland (Hatfield)-built B.35s converted to TT.35s. TW117 was a De Havilland (Leavesden)-built T.III. For static and taxi shots, TA642, RS718, TA724 (all TT.35s), TV959 a Leavesden-built T.III and TJ118 (TT.35) were assembled at Bovingdon. Of the five, TJ118 was found to be suitable for studio use and not taxiable, it was dismantled and the nose section taken to the MGM studio at Borehamwood in Hertfordshire. The wing section appears briefly in the film showing engineers at work.

Bovingdon makeover

Bovingdon was ideal for use as a film location; it was conveniently near Borehamwood and required little to convert it back to wartime configuration. Camouflage was applied to the buildings that would be in shot and a few minor conversions were carried out to parts of the airfield that would be used. The continued RAF presence may be seen on the big screen where one can detect Avro Ansons and Percival Pembrokes parked on the far side of the aerodrome. Also set up at Bovingdon was a small production line to alter the TT.35s and T.IIIs into mid-war configuration. This included the addition of four 0.303in Colt-Browning machine guns to the painted-over Perspex nose cone. While it was not ideal and does not look quite right, the expense of fabricating new nose sections with guns was not economical. Neither was the fitting of 20mm cannon troughs for accuracy and these were not proceeded with. While the aircraft had been operated by the CAACU at Exeter they wore an overall silver paint scheme, this was replaced with standard mid-Second World War camouflage and the squadron code letters 'HT' were added to the fuselage sides. In reality, these letters had been used by 154 and 601 Squadrons, both of which operated single-engine types.

While the Mosquitos were being worked on, Mahaddie was negotiating with the Spanish authorities for the lease of two or three Hispano HA-1112 fighters which were then still being operated by the Spanish Air Force. These Rolls-Royce Merlin-engined Messerschmitt Bf109s would be ideal for some of the action sequences in the film, but the fees quoted for the lease were too high and the deal fell through. Instead, two French-built Nord 1002 (copies of the Messerschmitt Bf108) F-BFYX and F-BGVU, were obtained and ferried to Bovingdon. They were given an overall olive drab colour scheme for use in the key rolls of bombing and airfield strafing. The special effects team, under Tom Howard, provided the necessary machine gun bursts and explosions as required. When filming was completed, the two Nords were sold in the United States to Gregory Board and Martin Caidin.

Gregory Board was involved with the

Still wearing its film serial, HJ898, and coded HT–G, this is actually B.35, TA719, which is today, preserved in CAACU period markings at the Imperial War Museum, Duxford. *Via Martyn Chorlton*

RF580 (RS712) undergoing some maintenance during the making of the film. The Mosquito was sold to the Strathallan Museum in 1972 but once the collection was forced to close, RS712 was bought by Kermit Weeks where it survives today, re-serialled N35MK. *Via Martyn Chorlton*

filming of *633 Squadron* as he supplied and piloted the North American B-25J Mitchell, N9089Z (ex-44-30861) that was used for aerial photography. His company, Aero Associates, based in Tucson, Arizona, had used the white and blue painted Mitchell as an executive transport and it was the ideal platform for filming. In one scene, the B-25 appears as an RAF aircraft and is seen taxying out and taking-off at night to drop an agent into occupied territory. For this brief sequence, RAF roundels were added and the registration shortened to N908 but the paint scheme was not changed.

Fiction based on fact

The story in the film differs from that of the book in many aspects; basically the film begins with a dramatic take-off by a Miles Messenger from Norway (Bovingdon) with a young naval officer on board. This is Lt Bergman, played by American actor George Chakiris, who has news of the heavy water plant buried deep underground and seemingly bomb proof. The allies know about the plant but cannot attack it due to its position, this is where Bergman's plans and 633 Squadron come in. Established stalwart actor Harry Andrews portrays an Air Marshal who proposes using the squadron to drop a new 'earthquake' bomb to blow-up the mountain above the factory entrance and bury the plant. Bergman will lead a group of resistance men to attack the enemy anti-aircraft positions enabling the Mosquitos to have a clear, low-level run up the fjord and drop their bombs on the target. Sqn Ldr Grant (Grenville in the book) will lead 633 Squadron on the mission. Naturally there is urgency and the squadron have just 17 days to train and launch the raid. Bergman is returned to Norway (via the B-25) but is captured before he can get to the resistance group and organize their part in the raid. Bergman is taken to Gestapo headquarters and tortured but does not divulge the plan; the Nazis find out about the raid and are able to kill members of the resistance in an ambush. Word of Bergman's capture reaches London and a mission to bomb the Gestapo building is put into action. Grant (Cliff Robertson) decides to fly the mission himself, even though he knows that he will kill Bergman in the process. Adding to the complication is that Grant has fallen for Bergman's sister (Austrian actress Maria Perschy) and has to tell her the news.

The late Cliff Robertson was excellent in the role of Grant and brought some authenticity to the part of a pilot as in real life he was a skilled and enthusiastic aviator. For many years he owned several aircraft including a Spitfire IX and flew it on a regular basis until he decided to retire from flying. Robertson appeared in several films and stage plays and ended his long career with a key supporting role in the first Spiderman film. Like so many films made in Britain, *633 Squadron* relies on the excellent character actors that this country used to specialize in. Apart from Harry Andrews, key roles were played by Donald Houston, Michael Goodliffe, Angus Lennie, John Mellion (who is Australian) and Johnny Briggs (later famous as Mike Baldwin in Coronation Street). When I spoke with some of those who had appeared in the film they all had happy memories of filming at Bovingdon and Borehamwood. Harry Andrews recalled that he *"did not have much to do with the aircraft, which were interesting to see but it was a happy unit and I had worked with many of the others in the past. I think the pilots who flew the aircraft enjoyed themselves!"* Angus Lennie, who was outstanding as Mac in *The Great*

TT.35 RS712 had a busy RAF career before it was purchased by Hamish Mahaddie for just £75 for the film. Originally built as a B.35, the Mosquito joined 13 OTU then, following conversion to a TT.35, served with 1 CAACU, Schleswigland TTF and 3/4 CAACU before being sold off. *Andy Hay/www.flyingart.co.uk*

Angus Lennie trying to pull Cliff Robertson out of a burning Mosquito at Borehamwood during the filming of *633 Sqn*. *Via author*

Escape also had fond memories, especially being taxied around the airfield in a Mosquito. *"We were not allowed to get airborne in them, I think the insurance people would not allow that. Would have been fun though!"*

On location

Most of the aerial filming was carried out in the Norfolk area which was not as crowded as the airspace around Bovingdon. For the 'enemy coast ahead' scenes, the overwater shots and the approaching coast are the Wash and Norfolk, these were from the nose camera position in the B-25. Cameras were also installed in the tail and side windows. Directors of Photography were Edward (Ted) Scaife and John Wilcox, both much respected and with several major film productions to their credit. Wilcox was largely responsible for the aerial footage.

Scotland was chosen for the training sequences and doubled as the Norway for the raid. Late in August 1963, while the main unit continued with principal photography at Bovingdon and Borehamwood, the second unit, under Wilcox, set off for Inverness (Dalcross) Airport with three Mosquitos, RS709, RS712, TA719, and the B-25. Pilots for Scotland were Crewdson, Hawke, Rich and Warden. Gregory Board had three cameras mounted in the nose, tail and starboard side of the B-25, with John Wilcox on board to direct the sequences.

Some of the training sequences were filmed on the Islew of Skye, but most of the other scenes were shot in and around Loch Morar, Loch Arkaig, Loch Lochy and Loch Ness. Bad weather hampered the unit and in the end they only had four or five days of good weather with clear visibility to get the aerial sequences completed. ❖

A rare image of Mosquito T.III TW117 during its RAF service, albeit as instructional airframe No.7895 with the School of Technical Training at Henlow. The aircraft was maintained in an airworthy condition and served as a conversion and refresher trainer for the pilots flying the Mosquito during the making of *633 Squadron*. *Via Martyn Chorlton* ▼

'Defending Norway against the RAF'. In a series of joint air exercises, the Royal Norwegian Air Force are defending their country, with British-built fighters, against raiding Lincoln and Lancaster bombers of the RAF. The bombers, thirty of them, are making mock day and night attacks from aerodromes in this country, without landing in Norway, in order to test the Norwegian defences. A Mosquito (FB.VI ex RS605 of 107 Sqn) of the Royal Norwegian Air Force flying over mountains where the snow persists all the year giving a good idea of the country they have to defend. *Charles E Brown via Aeroplane*

The Yugoslav Air Force (JRV) operated the Mosquito from 1951 until 1963, the same year that the type was retired in Britain. Of the 140 aircraft ordered, 60 of them were NF.38s, including ex-VX904 pictured in 1953 with the JRV serial 8010

Foreign Wings

Not including the Commonwealth countries of Australia, Burma, Canada, New Zealand and South Africa, the Mosquito was exported to thirteen other countries. David H Smith briefly covers those air forces.

Belgium

24 NF.30s were ordered by the Belgian Air Force in 1947 and, after being overhauled by Fairey Aviation at Ringway, were delivered as MB1 to MB24. Servicing of these aircraft was subsequently carried out by Avions Fairey at Gosselies. Further orders included at least eight T.IIIs, a pair of FB.VIs, a NF.XVII and a NF.XIX. The original NF.30s served with 10 and 11 Squadron of 1 Wing but following maintenance issues, all were grounded by 1953 although a few continued in service until 1956.

China

China was the largest export operator of the Mosquito. The Chinese Nationalist forces of Chiang Kai-shek ordered over 200 Canadian-built examples. The first aircraft were delivered in 1948 to Shanghai along with several de Havilland Canada technicians and pilots who would train the Chienese pilots on type. The majority of aircraft were FB.26s although at least one T.22 and several T.27s were also delivered. 1, 3 and 4 Squadrons of the Chinese Nationalist Forces flew the Mosquito, the majority seeing action against the Chinese communist forces.

Czechoslovakia

Following the reconstitution of the Czechoslovakian air force, one of the types chosen to rebuild it was the Mosquito. The Czechs needed a fighter bomber squadron and to equip it, 19 FB.VIs were chosen, redesignated as the B-36 and a few T.III trainers as well, redesignated as the CB-36. Deliveries began in 1947, the aircraft initially serving with the 'Atlantic Squadron' but, before the decade was over, the Czech Air Force was being re-organised into a Soviet system, so the unit became part of the 24th Air Regiment's first squadron aka, 1.letka, LP 24 or letecky pluk 24. Stationed at Pizen-Bory from 1949, the Mosquito was withdrawn in favour of Soviet types.

Dominican Republic

Delivery of five FB.VI's began in 1948 and three T.29s direct from Canada followed not long after. The type served until 1954.

France

The French Air Force or Armée de l'Air was by far the largest export operator of the Mosquito in Europe. More than 100 were ordered, 57 of these were FB.VIs, the remainder being made up of NF.30s and PR.XVIs. Deliveries began in 1945 to GC I/3 'Corse' (Groupe de Chasse) which was formed with FB.VIs in November 1945. By November 1946, GC I/3 was renumbered as GC I/6, later joined by a second unit operating the FB.VI, GC II/6 'Normandie-Niémen'.

Both units served in North Africa but, from 1947, GC I/6 operated in French Indo-China where the FB.VIs saw a great deal of action. By July 1949, the FB.VI had already been withdrawn from French service although the NF.30 and PR.XVI continued until June 1953. All French Mosquitoes wore their original RAF serials.

As NT330, this NF.30 served with 85 and 239 Squadrons before being transferred to the Belgian Air Force on December 21, 1948 as MB-20. The aircraft was not struck off strength until October 17, 1956

One the 19 FB.VIs supplied to the reconstituted Czech Air Force was ex-RF838 which originally served with 404 Squadron and 132 OTU. The aircraft was serialled IY-12 in Czech service, the 'IY' being the code letters for LP 24

Ex-TE612 was one of five FB.VIs supplied to the Dominican Air Force in 1943 and re-serialled as '301'

Israel

The number of Mosquitos that ended up in Israeli hands is uncertain. It is known that 68 ex-Armée de l'Air examples were delivered to Israel in June 1951 and, prior to this, a variety of marks, including the FB.VI, PR.XVI, NF.30, TR.33 and T.III were being operated.

The Mosquito proved to be a very valuable combat aircraft for the Israelis until mid-1956 when the type had to be withdrawn because of issues with the wood glue. A few were refurbished and put back into service in time for the Suez campaign in 1958.

Norway

A type that the Norwegians were more than familiar with thanks to its wartime operations, the Mosquito, joined the Royal Norwegian Air Force in November 1945 with 334 Squadron. An additional ten FB.VIs, three T.IIIs and a single B.35 for ground instructional use were later delivered to Norway. Two of the FB.VIs were converted with radar as temporary night-fighters but a fatal accident in 1951 saw the entire fleet grounded and, by January 1952, the Mosquito was removed from the Norwegian Air Force's inventory.

Soviet Union

A single Mosquito, B.IV Series II DK296 was supplied to the Soviets for evaluation by the Soviet Aircraft Research Institute. Despite being unimpressed with the worn out machine which had served with 105 Squadron, the Soviets gave serious consideration to licence building the aircraft. Apparently the Soviets had requested further Mosquitoes for evaluation but this was not forthcoming and on DK296's ninth flight, the aircraft was wrecked following undercarriage failure.

Sweden

In 1948, the Swedish Air Force ordered 60 NF.XIXs, the first of them, TA286 (re-serialled 30001) was delivered in July 1948. In Swedish service, the Mosquito was re-designated as the J.30, serving with the F.1 Fighter Wing. By 1954, several were removed from operational service because of structural failures and, by March 1955, the NF.XIX had made its last flight for the Swedish Air Force.

Switzerland

Neutral Switzerland inherited a pair of Mosquitoes during the Second World War, both of which had force-landed. The first was PR.IV DK310 of 1 PRU which force-landed on September 24, 1942 at Bern-Belp, becoming the first to fall in 'non-Allied' hands. The pilot, Flt Lt Wooll, attempted to burn the aircraft but the Swiss military arrived on the scene very quickly. Britain was very concerned that the aircraft could still fall into enemy hands and, on August 1, 1943, an agreement was made allowing Switzerland to operate the aircraft with the serial E-42. Initially used for flight testing by Swiss military pilots, the aircraft was later sold to Swissair in July 1944. By October, the aircraft was carrying out mail runs and, from January 1945, the Mosquito was serialled as HB-IMO. The aircraft was also used for instructional flights for Swissair pilots before being returning

All Mosquitoes that served with the Armée de l'Air retained their original RAF serials, including FB.VI RF616 which was supplied to the French on April 16, 1946

The four blade propellers and the arrestor hook give this Mosquito away as a TR.33, one of two aircraft, ex-TW237 or ex-TW238, that are connected with the serial 4x-3186. TW238 is known to have been delivered to the IDFAF (Israeli Defence Force Air Force) in July 1953

Mosquito FB.VI RS-650 which served the Royal Norwegian Air Force from 1945 to 1951

Mosquito B.IV DK296 was sent to the Soviet Union for evaluation in early 1944. Testing was carried out by the Soviet Aircraft Research Institute between April 25 and May 15, 1944. This is the aircraft on its final, unplanned, day of testing

The first of 60 Mosquito NF.XIXs for Sweden was the former TA286, which was originally supplied to the RAF, held in storage and then sold back to de Havilland on February 6, 1948

One of the first Mosquito FB.VIs delivered to the Turkish Air Force pictured at Gaziemir in 1947

Canadian-built USAAF F-8 Mosquito 334926 nicknamed *The Spook* which was originally built as KB315, a B.VII

A very rare image of a Yugoslav Air Force Mosquito FB.VI fitted with a torpedo whilst serving with the 21st Mixed Aviation Division

to the air force, which operated the aircraft until August 1946. The aircraft was then broken up for spares but was not deleted from the Swiss registry until July 1, 1951.

The second Mosquito to arrive unannounced in Switzerland was FB.VI, NS993 of 515 Squadron which force-landed at Dubendorf on September 30, 1944. The aircraft also served with Swiss Air Force specifically for the testing of the SM-1 jet engine which was mounted underneath the fuselage.

Turkey

Another large operator of the Mosquito was the Turkish Air Force which ordered approximately 120 FB.VIs and ten T.III(T) (Torpedo-Bomber) from January 1947. Three regiments were re-equipped with the Mosquito which was complete by April 1948.

The first unit to be established was the 3rd Regiment at Gaziemir for anti-shipping duties followed by the 1st Regiment at Eskişehir and the 2nd Regiment at Diyarbakir. Unfortunately, several accidents occurred through structural failure and this was attributed to old glue breaking down. By 1951, the 3rd Regiment had been disbanded while the 1st and 2nd Regiments were redesignated as the 1st and 2nd Air Base respectively. The Mosquito served the Turkish Air Force until the arrival of the F-84G Thunderjet in 1953.

United States

It was as early as 1942 that the United States began to show an interest in the Mosquito, to such an extent that, licenced production was seriously considered. Approximately 200 Mosquitoes, the majority of them the PR.XVI, went on to serve with the USAAF. The type was used for many specialist tasks including photographic recce, weather recce, night photography and target radar-scope photography using H2S. A few PR.XVIs operated by the 654th Bomb Squadron were equipped for communication with agents on the ground under code name Red Stocking.

By the summer of 1945, all surviving Mosquitoes were returned to the RAF including 40 Canadian-built B.XXs and B.IVs converted to the recce F-8 (43-34924 to 43-34963). The 416th Night Fighter Squadron, based in Italy, also flew the NF.30 from November 1944 to the end of the war.

Yugoslavia

Following a Yugoslavian delegation visiting Britain in 1951, orders were placed for 140 Mosquitoes, made up of 76 FB.VIs, 60 NF.38s and four T.IIIs. Deliveries began in 1951, the type serving with the 32nd Bombardment Division and the 21st Mixed Aviation Division. Some of the aircraft that served with the latter were modified to carry torpedoes. The type also served with the 103rd Reconnaissance Regiment and the 184th Reconnaissance Regiment, the former being used for training and conversion and the latter for operational duties. By mid-1960, the type had been virtually withdrawn although a few Mosquitoes were used as target-tugs until 1963.

Speedbirds across the North Sea

Between 1942 and late 1944, the superior performance of the Mosquito made it ideal for clandestine operations to and from Sweden.

A BOAC–operated Mosquito FB.VI on finals at Leuchars, Fife on return from a 'Courier Run' from Sweden, circa 1944. *Aeroplane*

BOAC (British Overseas Airways Company) and the Mosquito

BOAC HAD ALREADY been flying a 'special air service' from Leuchars to Stockholm since 1941. The flight was also known as the 'ball-bearing run' because of the precious cargo that was being purchased from Sweden. These early flights across the North Sea were carried out by the Lockheed 14 but, by mid-1942, the Mosquito, with its superior performance, was suggested as a replacement.

On August 5, 1942, a Mosquito belonging to 105 Squadron carried out a trial run from Leuchars to Stockholm, covering the 800 miles in less than three hours. The type was clearly suited to this type of high-speed long-distance operation but it was not until December 15, 1942 when the first Mosquito, ex-DZ411, re-registered as G-AGFV, was delivered to BOAC.

The first official BOAC Mosquito flight to Stockholm was carried out on February 4, 1943 and by May the airline had six Mosquitoes on strength not including a T.III on hand for conversion and refresher training.

Ball-bearings were not the only cargo brought back from Sweden because the bomb bay of several of BOAC's Mosquitoes was converted to a carry a passenger. The bay was line with plywood and padded with felt, fuel pipes were diverted and a safety harness was fitted. The passenger would have to wear a lined flying suit for protection against the extreme cold and a personal oxygen mask and supply were also provided. The passenger also had an electric light and, on departure, a thermos flask of coffee or tea was issued and sometimes sandwiches for the VIPs.

Early flights to Sweden were flown in daylight but after a few near misses the majority were switched to night time. Out of the ten Mosquitoes that served BOAC during this period, six of them were lost; two of them crashed in Sweden, two in the North Sea and two more whilst approaching Leuchars. The last operational Mosquito flight was carried out on November 30, 1944, the task being taken over by the Douglas DC-3. ✤

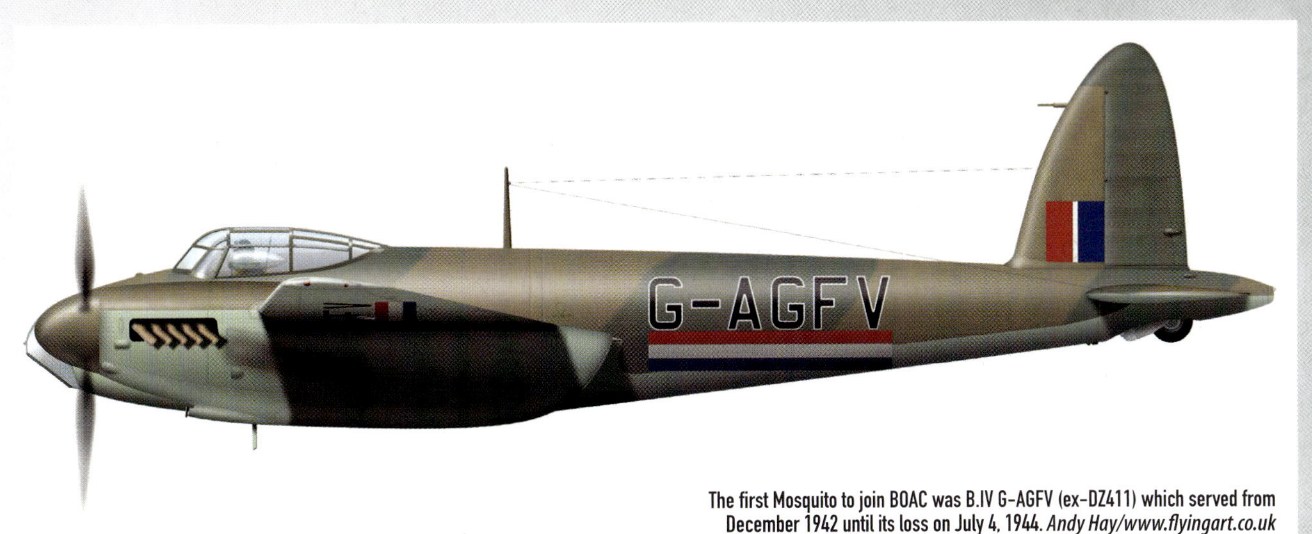

The first Mosquito to join BOAC was B.IV G-AGFV (ex-DZ411) which served from December 1942 until its loss on July 4, 1944. *Andy Hay/www.flyingart.co.uk*

G-AGGD on finals to land at Leuchars in late 1943 was a new-build FB.VI built at Hatfield and delivered to the RAF in April 1943. The Mosquito only served with BOAC until its demise at Sarenas, Sweden, on January 3, 1944. *Via Martyn Chorlton* ➤

BOAC MOSQUITOES

G-AGFV   ex-DZ411 B.IV. Crashed near Stockholm on July 4, 1944.
G-AGGC   ex-HJ680 FB.VI. Returned to RAF.
G-AGGD   ex-HJ681 FB.VI. Crashed Sarenas, Sweden, on January 3, 1944.
G-AGGE   ex-HJ718 FB.VI. Returned to RAF.
G-AGGF   ex-HJ720 FB.VI. Crashed Ester Balloch Hill, Glenlee, Invermairk, Angus on August 17, 1943.
G-AGGG   ex-HJ721 FB.VI. Crashed on landing at Leuchars on October 25, 1943.
G-AGGH   ex-HJ723 FB.VI. Returned to RAF.
G-AGKO   ex-HJ667 FB.VI. Returned to RAF.
G-AGKP   ex-LR296 FB.VI. Crashed into North Sea off Leuchars on August 19, 1944.
G-AGKR   ex-HJ792 FB.VI. Lost between Gothenburg and Leuchars on August 29, 1944.

Trainers operated by BOAC

HJ885   T.III.
HJ898   T.III. April 1945 to May 1945.
HJ985   T.III. November 1943 to January 1944.
LR524   T.III. February 1944 to December 1944.

▲ Ex-HJ721 was another FB.VI that only served with BOAC. Given the civilian registration G-AGGG, the Mosquito was written off in a crash at Leuchars on October 25, 1943. *Via Martyn Chorlton*

-HMT

Spartan Air Services Mosquito PR.35 CF-HMT was originally built as B.35 (RS711) which served with 139 and 109 Squadrons before being sold to the Canadian-based company for conversion to the high altitude mapping role on December 15, 1954. *Mike Hooks*

Mosquito T.3 RR299 was probably the most well-known flying Mosquito — so far! Built at Hatfield in early 1945, '299 flew with a host of RAF units until March 14, 1963 when the aircraft was retired to 27 MU at Shawbury. RR299 was then purchased by Hawker Siddeley and by 1965 was re-registered as G-ASKH, though it never displayed this registration. The aircraft is pictured during the late 1960s with Hawarden-based chief test pilot Tony Craig at the controls. She was lost in a tragic accident at Barton on July 21, 1996, when the pilot lost control after losing power to the port engine during a steep wing over. The pilot, Kevin Moorhouse, who had less than five hours on the Mosquito, and his engineer Steve Watson, both died in the ensuing crash. *Aeroplane*

Long and loyal service

▲ 139 Squadron was one of the earliest units to receive the Mosquito in 1942 and continued to operate the type until it re-equipped with the English Electric Canberra in November 1952. Two of the unit's Mosquito B.35s are receiving some attention at Hemswell, Lincolnshire, circa 1950. *Aeroplane*

After being disbanded on August 31, 1945, by the following day, 4 Squadron was reformed and re-equipped with the Mosquito FB.IV at Volkel in West Germany. The unit was continually on the move within Germany during the FB.IV's service, although it is believed that this image was taken at Celle in December 1949. *FLIGHT via Aeroplane*

MOSQUITO PR.I - 1 PRU (Photographic Reconnaissance Unit), 8 OTU (Operational Training Unit), 69*, 521, 540, AAEE, PRU

MOSQUITO NF.II - 1 FPP (Ferry Pilots Pool), 1 FTU (Ferry Training Unit), 1 PRU, 1 OADU (Overseas Aircraft Despatch Unit), 1 RS (Radio School), 8 OTU, 13 OTU, 16 OTU, 19 MU (Maintenance Unit), 23, 25, 27, 51 OTU, 54 OTU, 60 OTU, 85, 105, 132 OTU, 140, 141, 143, 151, 157, 169, 239, 264, 301 FTU, 307, 333, 339, 410, 418, 455, 456, 515, 605, 681, 684, 1422 Flt, 1692 CU (Conversion Unit), 1692 Flt (Flight), AAEE (Aeroplane & Armament Experimental Establishment), BSDU (Bomber Support Development Unit), DH (de Havilland), FE (Far East), FIU (Fighter Interception Unit), Hdlg Sqn (Handling Squadron), Hunsdon SF (Station Flight), Malta SF, ME (Middle East), OADU, RAE (Royal Aircraft Establishment), Rolls-Royce, SHAEF CS (Supreme Headquarters Allied Expeditionary Force Communication Squadron), TFU (Telecommunications Flying Unit)

MOSQUITO T.III - 1 CAACU (Civilian Anti-Aircraft Co-Operation Unit), 1 FU (Ferry Unit), 1 OFU (Overseas Ferry Unit), 2 APS (Armament Practice Station), 3 & 3-4 CAACU, 4, 4 FP, 6 OTU, 8, 8 OTU, 13, 13 OTU, 14,16 OTU, 19, 25, 29, 33, 36, 39, 41, 45, 58, 51 OTU, 54 OTU, 60 OTU, 64, 80, 81, 98, 109, 132 OTU, 139, 141, 180, 199, 204 AFS (Advanced Flying School), 204 CTU (Combat/Crew Training Unit), 219, 226 OCU (Operational Conversion Unit), 228 OCU, 231 OCU, 264, 489, 500, 502, 504, 605, 608, 609, 616, 1330 CU, 1655 MTU (Mosquito Training Unit), 1689 Flt, A&AEE, APS (Armament Practice Station) Lubeck , ATF (Armament Training Flight) Celle, Bassingbourn SF, BCIS (Bomber Command Instructors School), BCOCU (Bomber Command OCU), Celle SF, CFE (Central Fighter Establishment), CFS (Central Flying School), Church Fenton SF, Coltishall SF, Coningsby SF, ECFS (Empire Central Flying School), ETPS (Empire Test Pilots School, Eastleigh SF, Fassberg SF, FCCS (Fighter Command Communication Squadron), FE, FETS (Far East Training Squadron), FTU, HCEU (Home Command Examining Unit), Hemswell SF, Institute of Aviation Medicine, Ismailia SF, Leuchars SF, Linton SF, Luneburg SF, Manston SF, MCU (Mosquito Conversion Unit), ME, MTU, Pershore SF, Swinderby SF, Sylt SF, Tangmere SF, Wahn SF, West Malling SF, Wing Leader 136 Wing, Wittering SF

MOSQUITO B.IV - 1 OADU, 1 PRU, 8 OTU, 13 OTU, 16 OTU, 105, 106, 109, 138 Wg (Wing), 139, 140 Wg, 169, 192, 256, 305 FTU, 418, 521, 540, 544, 605, 618, 627, 683, 692, 1401 Flt, 1404 Flt, 1409 Flt, 1473 Flt, 1474 Flt, 1655 CU, 1655 MTU, AAEE, AFDU (Air Fighting Development Unit), Banff SF, BDU (Bomber Development Unit), Benson SF, BOAC (British Overseas Aircraft Corporation), FIU, Lyneham SF, Manston SF, Marham SF, MAEE (Maritime Aircraft Experimental Establishment), ME, NTU (Navigation Training Unit, Pathfinder Force), PRDU (Photographic Reconnaissance Development Unit), RAE, TFU, Turnhouse SF, Vickers

MOSQUITO FB.VI - 1 FP, 1 FU, 1 MECCU (Middle East Check & Conversion Unit), 1 OADU, 1 OFU, 1 Prep Pool, 2 APS, 2 FU, 2 Gp CF (Group Communication Flight), 2 Gp CS, 2 GSU (Ground Support Unit), 3 ADF (Aircraft Delivery Flight), 3 FP, 3 FPP, 4, 5 FU, 6

81 Squadron re-formed as a PR unit at Seletar on September 1, 1946, their equipment being the Spitfire PR.XIX and the Mosquito PR.34. The latter remained in service until December 1955. This is PR.34A RG177 which served the squadron until March 17, 1955 when the Mosquito swung on landing and the undercarriage was raised to stop the aircraft. *Andy Hay/www.flyingart.co.uk*

The famous night-fighter unit, 85 Squadron, operated seven different variants of the Mosquito between August 1942 and October 1951. The type was replaced by the Meteor NF.11. These are the unit's final variant, the NF.36, at rest at West Malling in 1947. *Via Martyn Chorlton*

After receiving the Mosquito B.IV in November 1941, 105 Squadron re-equipped with the B.IX at Marham in June 1943 while part of 8 Group, Pathfinder Force. LR507 was one of the lucky aircraft that survived the Second World War only to be SOC May 15, 1946. *Andy Hay/www.flyingart.co.uk*

109 Squadron was reformed in December 1940 as a heavy bomber unit, initially operating the Whitley, the Wellington and then the Lancaster. The unit received the Mosquito from December 1942 by which time it was serving with 8 Group at Wyton. *Via Martyn Chorlton*

FP, 6 OTU, 7 FPP, 8, 8 ARU (Aircraft Repair Unit), 8 FU, 8 OTU, 9 FU, 9 RFU (Refresher Flying Unit), 10 FU, 11, 12 FU, 13 ARU, 13 OTU, 14, 15 FPP, 16, 16 FU, 16 OTU, 18, 21, 21 FC, 22, 22 FC, 23, 25, 25 APC, 27, 27 MU, 29, 36, 39, 44 MU, 45, 46, 47, 51 MU, 51 OTU, 54 OTU, 58 MU, 59 SP , 60 OTU, 69, 82, 84, 84 Gp CS (Group Communication Squadron), 85, 89, 102 FRS (Flying Refresher Squadron), 107, 108, 109, 110, 114, 132 OTU, 138 Wg CU (Wing Communication Unit), 141, 142 RSU (Repair & Salvage Unit), 143, 143 RSU, 151, 151 RU (Repair Unit), 157, 162, 169, 192, 201 AFS, 204 AFS, 204 AGS (Air Gunners School), 204 APS, 211, 216 Gp CF, 228 OCU, 231 OCU, 235, 239, 248, 251, 256, 264, 268, 301 FTU, 304 FTU, 305, 307, 308 MU, 315 MU, 333, 334, 390 MU, 404, 410, 417, 417 RSU, 418, 451, 456, 464, 487, 489, 515, 540, 605, 613, 617, 618, 681, 682, 684, 1300 Flt, 1330 CU,1331 FTU, 1409 Flt,1672 CU, 1692 Flt, AAEE, ACSEA (Air Command South East Asia), ADU (Aircraft Delivery Unit), AEAF CF (Allied Expeditionary Air Forces Communication Flight), AFDS (Air Fighting Development Squadron), AFDU, Airspeed, APS Acklington, ASWDU (Air-Sea Warfare Development Unit), ATDU (Air Torpedo Development Unit), BAFO Com Wg (British Air Forces of Occupation Communications Wing), Benson SF, BOAC, BSDU, Buckeburg SF, CCDU (Coastal Command Development Unit), CFE, CGS (Central Gunnery School), CRD (Controller of Research & Development) Ansty, CRE (Central Reconnaissance Establishment), CS(A) (Controller of Supplies (Air)), CSE (Central Signals Establishment), Defford SF, DH, EAAS (Empire Air Armament School), ECFS, EFS (Empire Flying School), ETPS, FCAP, FCCS, FE, FIDS (Fighter Interception Development Squadron), FIU, GATU (Ground Attack Training Unit), Hdlg Sqn, Malta SF, Lubeck SF, ME, Med, NEI CS (Netherlands East Indies Communication Squadron), NFDW (Night Fighter Development Wing), North Creake SF, Northolt SF, OFU, Pershore SF, Polebrook SF, RAE, Rolls-Royce, RWE (Radio Warfare Establishment), SDU (Signals Development Unit), Swinderby SF, TFU, TRE, Vickers, West Raynham SF

MOSQUITO PR.VIII - 8 OTU, 85, 540, AAEE, Turnhouse SF

MOSQUITO B.IX - 105, 109, 139, 571, 627, 1317 Flt, 1409 Flt, AAEE, ATDU, BDU, DH, Hdlg Sqn, Little Snoring SF, Marham SF, ME, Oulton SF, RAE, TFU, TRE, Wyton SF

MOSQUITO PR.IX - 8 OTU, 105, 109, 140, 205 Gp, 256, 309 FTU, 317 MU, 454, 540, 541, 544, 614, 627, 680, 681, 684, 1317 Flt, 1409 Flt, DH, FE, FIU, ME, PRDU, RAE, Rolls-Royce, Wickenby SF

MOSQUITO NF.XII - 29, 51 OTU, 54 OTU, 85, 86 Gp CS, 96, 108, 151, 155 MU, 219, 256, 264, 286, 307, 406, 410, 488, 604, 1422 Flt, 1692 Flt, AAEE, CFE, CGS, Colerne SF, Defford SF, DH, FIDS, FIU, Heston SF, Horsham St Faith SF, Malta SF, TFU

MOSQUITO NF. XIII - 1 FU, 3 FU, 4 FU, 13 MU, 29, 51 OTU, 54 OTU, 85, 85 Gp CS, 96, 108, 151, 196, 218 MU, 256, 264, 301 FTU, 304 FTU, 307, 409, 410, 488, 604, CGS, DH, FIU, Malta SF, ME, NFDU (Night Fighter Development Unit), RAE, TRE

MOSQUITO NF.XV (EXPAND) - 8 OTU, 85, 540, 1409 Flt, Turnhouse SF

MOSQUITO B.XVI - 3 FP, 4, 5 FP, 14, 16 OTU, 27 MU, 44 MU, 69, 98, 105, 109, 128, 139, 140, 151 RU, 163,

169, 176, 180, 192, 195, 204 CTU, 231 OCU, 256, 274 MU, 333, 400, 540, 544, 571, 578, 608, 618, 627, 680, 684, 692, 1317 Flt, 1409 Flt, 1655 MTU, AAEE, BBU (Bomb Ballistics Unit), BDU, BTU, CBE (Central Bomber Establishment), CSE, DH, EANS (Empire Air Navigation School), GAL (General Aircraft Ltd), Henlow SF, SFU (Signals Flying Unit), RAE, Rotol, RWE, TFU, Upwood SF, West Freugh SF, Woodbridge SF, Woodhall Spa SF

MOSQUITO NF.XVII - 25, 51 OTU, 54 OTU, 68, 85, 125, 157, 219, 456, CBE, CFE, CFS, DH, FIU, Little Snoring SF, NFDU, NFDW, RAE, SIU (Signals Intelligence Unit), TRE, West Raynham SF

MOSQUITO FB.XVIII - 248, 254, 618, AAEE, DH

MOSQUITO NF.XIX - 1 OADU, 3 & 12 FU, 13 MU, 51 & 54 OTU, 68, 85, 89, 144 MU, 157, 162 MU, 169, 176, 235, 239, 255, 256, 257, 500, 600, 605, 609, 1550 CU, 1653 CU, 1660 CU, 1668 CU, 1692 Flt, BSDU, DH, FE, FIDS, ME, RAE, TFU

MOSQUITO B.XX/B.20 - 3 FPP, 16 OTU, 45 Gp, 105, 109, 112 Wg, 128, 139, 162, 163, 608, 627, 692, 1655 MTU, AAEE, Castle Kennedy SF, NTU, RAE, Rolls-Royce, Scottish Aviation, Upwood SF

MOSQUITO B.XXV/B.25 - 1 OAFU, 5 FP, 5 Gp Film Unit, 13 MU, 16 OTU, 24, 45 Gp, 109, 112 Wg, 128, 139, 142, 162, 163, 502, 571, 608, 614, 627, 692, 1655 MTU, ADLS (Air Delivery Letter Service), ATTDU (Air Transport Tactical Development Unit), BDU, ECFS, EFS, FE, ME, NTU, RAE, TCDU (Transport Command Development Unit), Upwood SF

MOSQUITO FB.26 - 1 FU, 3 FP, 6 FU, 10 MU, 13 MU, 29, 39, 45 Gp, 55, 49, 151, 249, AAEE, DH, Little Snoring SF, Med (Mediterranean), Polebrook SF, RAE

MOSQUITO NF.XXX/NF.30 - 1 ADF, 1 FU, 1 OADU, 4 FU, 5 MU, 10 MU, 12 FU, 15 MU, 23, 25, 29, 44 MU, 51 MU, 51 OTU, 54 OTU, 68, 85, 96, 125, 141, 151, 157, 219, 228 OCU, 239, 255, 264, 307, 406, 410, 456, 488, 500, 502, 504, 605, 608, 609, 616, AAEE, BSDU, CFE, CS(A), CSE, DH, ECFS, Gatwick SF, ME, Med, NFDU, NFDW, RAE, Rolls-Royce, RWE, TFU, Vickers-Armstrongs

MOSQUITO PR.XXXII/PR.32 - 540, 544, AAEE, DH

SEA MOSQUITO TR.33 - ECFS Handling Sqn Hullavington, MAEE, Highball Trials Flt Coningsby

MOSQUITO PR.XXXIV/PR.34 - 1 FU, 1 OADU, 1 OFU, 8 OTU, 9 MU, 13, 18, 27 MU, 51 MU, 58, 81, 107 MU, 111 OTU, 192, 231 OCU, 237 OCU, 308 MU, 540, 544, 680, 681, 684, AAEE, APDU, Bassingbourn SF, BEA, CSE, DH, FCCS, FE, KCS, Leuchars SF, Met Flt, Met Res Flt, OFU, Oulton SF, PRDU, RAE, RCASU, Rotol, SIU, TFU

MOSQUITO PR.34A - 58, 81, 192, 231 OCU, 237 OCU, 540, CSE

MOSQUITO XXXV/B.35 - 3 FP, 5 CAACU, 13 OTU, 14, 23, 38 MU, 98, 109, 139, 142, 230 OCU, 231 OCU, 527, AAEE, AFEE, APDU (Air Photography Development Unit), ATDU, Bassingbourn SF, BBU, BTU, CBE, Celle SF, Coningsby SF, CSE, DH, EANS, ECFS, ETPS, General Aircraft, Hemswell SF, Luneburg SF, ML Engineering, PRDU, RAE, SIU

MOSQUITO PR.35 - 11 OFU, 58, AAEE, Benson SF

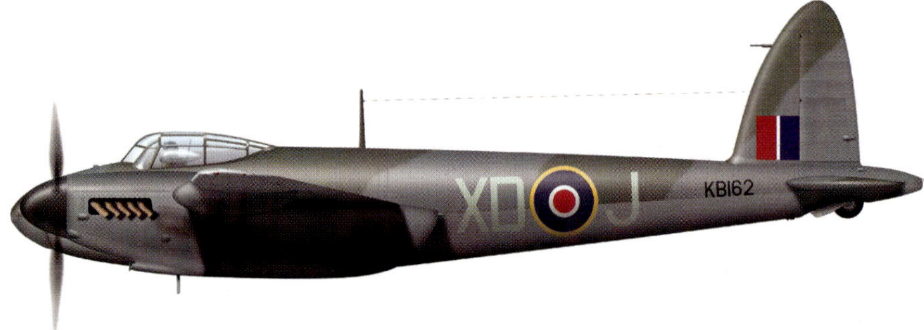

▲ 139 Squadron operated three different marks simultaneously during 1943 and 1944 including the B.XX. KB162 served the unit from late 1943 until October 14, 1944 when the aircraft had to be force-landed after an engine failed following take off from Warboys. *Andy Hay/www.flyingart.co.uk*

▲ Reformed with the Mosquito B.XXV at Bourn, in December 1944, 162 Squadron saw out the last few months of the war serving with 8 Group. *Andy Hay/www.flyingart.co.uk*

▲ Mosquito FB.VI TA588 of the Central Gunnery School, one of 13 operating with the school which was based at Leconfield from 1945 to 1954. *Via Martyn Chorlton*

▲ Sea Mosquito TR.33, TW241 which served with 778 Squadron, the TRE, RAE, 703 and 771 Squadron. *Via Martyn Chorlton*

▲ 617 Squadron operated four Mosquito FB.VIs, NS992, NS993, NT202 and NT205. NT202 broke up in mid-air over Wainfleet during a dive bombing practice attack on August 7, 1944. *Andy Hay/www.flyingart.co.uk*

▲ Formed at Skitten in March 1943, 618 Squadron was selected to use the Barnes Wallis designed 'Highball', a smaller, spherical version of his bouncing bomb, designed for attacking enemy warships. *Andy Hay/www.flyingart.co.uk*

▲ Formed specifically to serve with 8 Group, 692 Squadron was formed at Graveley in January 1944 and disbanded at Gransden Lodge by September 1945. The unit flew the Mosquito B.IV and B.XVI, including MM183. *Andy Hay/www. flyingart.co.uk*

▲ The pilots of 3 CAACU at Exeter, pictured not long after the unit was formed on March 18, 1951 in front of a Mosquito TT.35. On July 1, 1954, the unit was amalgamated with 4 CAACU to become 3/4 CAACU. Chief Pilot Harry Ellis is in the middle of the front row. *Via Aeroplane*

*All number only entries relate to a squadron

MOSQUITO TT.35 - 1 & 2 CAACU, 2 TAF CS, 3, 3-4 & 4 CAACU, 4 FP, 5 CAACU, 223 OCU, 226 OCU, 228 OCU, 229 OCU, 233 OCU, 236 OCU, 238 OCU, AAEE, Aldergrove SF, APS Sylt, Ballykelly SF, Gibraltar TTF (Target Towing Flight), Hdlg Sqn Kinloss SF, Schleswigland SF, St Eval TTF, Thum Flt Woodvale (Temperature & Humidity), TTF

MOSQUITO XXXVI/NF.36 - 22 MU, 23, 25, 29, 39, 85, 131, 141, 199, 219, 228 OCU, 230 OCU, 264, CFE, Coltishall SF, CSE, DH, FIDS, Manby SF, NFDS (Night Fighter Development Squadron), RAE, TFU, Vickers-Armstrongs, Wattisham SF, West Malling SF

MOSQUITO NF.38 - AAEE, AIEU, CFE, Hdlg Sqn, RAE, TFU, TRE

SEA MOSQUITO TT.39 - 51 MU, 274 MU, AFEE (Airborne Forces Experimental Establishment), RAE

MOSQUITO NF.II - HMS *Triumph*, NAD/RAE

MOSQUITO T.III - 762, 780, AHU (Aircraft Holding Unit) Abbotsinch, Lossiemouth & Stretton, Airwork Brawdy & St Davids, Brooklands Aviation, Culdrose, Fleetlands, Ford, MTCE, RDU Culham, Test Flt Stretton,

MOSQUITO FB.VI - 703, 704, 751, 762, 771, 778, 780, 787, 790, 811, 881, AHU Lossiemouth & Stretton, RDU Culham, RNARY (Royal Navy Aircraft Repair Yard) Fleetlands

MOSQUITO NF.XIII - 10 MU (RNDA), HMS *Triumph*, NAD/RAE

MOSQUITO B.XVI - 728, 771, A&AEE ('C' Flt), AHU Culdrose, Lossiemouth & Stretton, GAL Feltham/Lasham, RNAY Fleetlands

MOSQUITO PR.XVI - 274 MU, 728, 770, 771, 772, AHU Culham, Hal Far, Lossiemouth & Stretton, Airwork FRU (Fleet Requirements Unit) Hurn, Brooklands Aviation, RDU Culham, RNARY Fleetlands, Yeovilton

MOSQUITO B.25 - 728, 733, 762, 770, 771, 772, 777, 778, 790, 794, 827, AHU Bramcote, Hal Far & Stretton, Brawdy, NARIU Middle Wallop, RAE

MOSQUITO NF.30 - GI (Ground Instruction) only at RNAS (Royal Naval Air Station) Arbroath & Yeovilton

SEA MOSQUITO TR.33 - 703, 739, 751, 762, 771, 778, 787, 790, 811, AAEE ('C' & 'D' Flt), Airwork Brawdy, FRU (Hurn) & St Davids, AHU Lossiemouth & Stretton, ARS Ford, ATDU Gosport & Stretton, ECFS, FRU, MAEE ('Highball'), NARIU Stretton, RAE, RDU Culham, RN Section (RAF Defford), RNARY Fleetlands, TRE, TREFU

MOSQUITO PR.34 - 751, 771, 772, AHU Lossiemouth & Stretton, Brooklands Aviation, NARIU Gosport, RDU Culham,

SEA MOSQUITO TR.37 - 703, AHU Lossiemouth & Stretton, RAE, RDU Culham

SEA MOSQUITO TT.39 - 771, 728, AAEE, AHU Culdrose, Lossiemouth & Stretton, GAL Feltham/Lasham

'In 1940 I could at least fly as far as Glasgow in most of my aircraft, but not now! It makes me furious when I see the Mosquito. I turn green and yellow with envy. The British, who can afford aluminium better than we can, knock together a beautiful wooden aircraft that every piano factory over there is building, and they give it a speed which they have now increased yet again.

What do you make of that? There is nothing the British do not have. They have the geniuses and we have the nincompoops. After the war is over I'm going to buy a British radio set – then at least I'll own something that has always worked.'

Hermann Göring, 1943.